"This is a much-needed reminder that gospel Christianity thrives when it is out of power, and that Christian courage comes from trusting not in cultural power but in God's power and grace."

TIMOTHY KELLER, Founding Pastor, Redeemer Presbyterian Church, Manhattan; author of *Making Sense of God*

"We live in an age of increasing hostility toward Christianity in the West. These are days that will require courage, conviction, and clarity of vision. Matt Chandler's new book, *Take Heart*, is a thoughtful, pastoral, and brave call for faithfulness in a trying time. These pages are filled with practical wisdom and sound theological principles that fuel courage in the face of opposition."

R. ALBERT MOHLER, JR., President of the Southern Baptist Theological Seminary

"In *Take Heart*, Matt Chandler offers both challenge and comfort to Christians in an age where both are desperately needed. He speaks with both a prophet's urgency and a pastor's heart, and this book will serve all Christians who are wondering how we navigate the troubled waters of our present age."

MIKE COSPER, Executive Director, Harbor Media; author of *Recapturing the Wonder*

"Fearing, agonizing, retreating, embracing. These are a few of the responses we see and might be experiencing in a 'post-Christian' culture. Chandler knows how many of us feel in our current cultural moment in the West. Through biblical truth, Chandler helps redirect our eyes to the One who can strengthen and encourage us so we might have courage."

TRILLIA NEWBELL, author of *God's Very Good Idea* and *Enjoy*

"As Christians, we are defined not as a people of fear but a people of hope. Matt Chandler has written a timely book that encourages, inspires, and equips believers to walk in that hope in our current culture. This is an excellent resource for every believer desiring to live as 'salt and light' in today's world."

MATT CARTER, Pastor of Preaching, The Austin Stone Community Church, Austin

"This is a deeply encouraging book. I mean that literally: it brings courage to the reader. It is also enjoyably punchy, readably short, practically wise, and pastorally insightful, with a warmth and winsomeness that books on this subject sometimes lack. Get hold of a copy, and be en-*courage*-d."

ANDREW WILSON, Teaching Pastor, King's Church London

"Matt Chandler is a man of courage and conviction. He is gifted with a prophetic voice, pointing the church and the world toward the beauty of the gospel, and calling upon Christians to live faithfully in the world. *Take Heart* is a sign of that message—that Christians can live courageously because Jesus is alive."

RUSSELL MOORE, President of the Ethics and Religious Liberty Commission of the Southern Baptist Convention; author of *Onward*

"How do we engage a culture steeped in secularism? A fear-based operating system invoking a fight-or-flight response has proven to be historically insufficient. Instead we need a cohort of winsomely courageous Christ-followers to show us the way forward: the kind of person Matt Chandler has proven himself to be, and that he writes about in *Take Heart*."

BRYAN LORITTS, Lead Pastor, Abundant Life Church, Silicon Valley; author of *Saving the Saved*

"For many of us, these seem hard days indeed to be a Christian. But by reminding us of the church's long, rich history and of God's strong, constant love, *Take Heart* shows us that even in this difficult age, believers have every reason for courage and to be of good cheer."

KAREN SWALLOW PRIOR, author of *Fierce Convictions: The Extraordinary Life of Hannah More: Poet, Reformer, Abolitionist*

"Matt is a voice I trust. In times of significant cultural shift in the world, we need courage. Instead of walking in fear and making false proclamations about the church's mortality, we must brace ourselves for a deeper sense of commitment to courageous engagement. Pick up this book to get pointed in the right direction, and walk in commitment to strategic courage in this time of shifting uncertainty."

ERIC MASON, Founder and Lead Pastor, Epiphany Fellowship, Philadelphia

"Countless Christians today have simply given up or lost hope. If that sounds like you, Matt Chandler has a word to speak: it's a great time to be a Christian; be courageous; take heart. If that sounds hollow and naïve, you need to read this book. Matt is keenly in touch with the troubles we face but even more so with the Lord of the universe, who ultimately wins. What he advocates isn't a fleshly triumphalism but a courageous faith in a really big God. *Take Heart* speaks a hopeful and thoroughly biblical word that all of us need to hear. Highly recommended!"

SAM STORMS, Lead Pastor, Bridgeway Church, Oklahoma City; President of the Evangelical Theological Society

"Do not be dismayed, for this is not the first time the very heart of God's plan for his people and his world has been questioned, assaulted, and pushed to the margins. This is the central message of this timely book by my dear brother Matt. Yet there is more. Within these pages you will be challenged to think critically about where your hope is actually invested, how you view the church's role with respect to the state, and if you indeed love you neighbor as yourself. Take heart: you are alive in an age ripe with opportunity and you can actually be integral to changing the world!"

LÈONCE B. CRUMP JR., Founding Pastor, Renovation Church, Atlanta; author of *Renovate: Changing Who You Are by Loving Where You Are*

"What a wonderful, inspiring work! In a time where Christianity is said to be losing ground in the culture, our impulse may be to panic. But what if this were actually our most opportune moment to experience renewal, and to become the kind of life-giving, world-changing disciples Jesus has always intended for us to be? In characteristic fashion, Matt has done a terrific job of laying out such a vision. In so doing, he has gotten me excited about the many things God still wants to do in the world, and the part we can all play in his plan."

SCOTT SAULS, Senior Pastor, Christ Presbyterian Church, Nashville; author of *Jesus Outside the Lines, Befriend,* and *From Weakness to Strength*

TAKE
HEART

The Village
Church Resources™

Take Heart *Christian Courage in the Age of Unbelief*
© 2018 The Village Church

Published by
The Good Book Company
Tel (US): 866 244 2165
Tel (UK): 0333 123 0880
Email (US): info@thegoodbook.com
Email (UK): info@thegoodbook.co.uk

Websites:
North America: www.thegoodbook.com
UK: www.thegoodbook.co.uk
Australia: www.thegoodbook.com.au
New Zealand: www.thegoodbook.co.nz

Design by The Good Book Company / The Village Church

ISBN: 9781784983161 | Printed in Denmark

To The Village Church.

You were on our hearts when we were writing this book.
May we have many more years of ministry together.

CONTENTS

1. WE CAN THRIVE

For the church, the skies are growing dark in the West. But the sky is not falling in.

In fact, this is a great time to be a Christian.

I know it may not look like that. From terrorist attacks to racial injustice to political chaos to an increasingly secular world that seems to have lost its moral center, we find ourselves in some unique and challenging times. Fear runs rampant across our cultural landscape—and, especially and increasingly, fear sits in the pews of our churches. Talk to most Christians—or read most Christian blogs and social-media streams—and it's clear that the church isn't what it was. Or rather, it isn't where it was.

What do I mean? Bernie Sanders will explain for me. In spring 2017, the Vermont senator, who came closer than anyone expected to winning the Democratic nomination for U.S. President in 2016, discovered that Russell Vought, deputy director of the Office of Management and Budget, holds to the orthodox Christian belief on salvation—and that, therefore, he believes that Muslims are "condemned."

Here is what Sanders said in Vought's Senate confirmation hearing:

"It is hateful, it is Islamophobic, and it is an insult to over a billion Muslims throughout the world ... This country, since its inception, has struggled, sometimes with great pain, to overcome discrimination of all forms ... we must not go backwards."

Welcome to the age of unbelief.

Unless you want to place your head in the sand and leave it there, there's no denying the fact that fewer and fewer people are claiming to be Christians throughout the West, and that Christians are losing social status and favor more and more, almost by the day.

For those in the United States, we're seeing "Christian America" pass away right before our eyes. Our "one nation under God" doesn't look and feel that way anymore. Many European nations are way downstream from there. It's the end of the age of Christendom.

Whether it's legislation around issues such as gay marriage and transgender identities... or the debates around what religious liberty really is (and whether it even matters)... or the popularity of the "new atheists" like Richard Dawkins and Sam Harris... or just the way our neighbors and co-workers look at us if we mention that we agree with what Christ said about salvation, relationships, or truth... we're in a new era.

It was one thing to move toward a pluralistic society, where we lived among those who looked and thought differently than us, and who believed differently than us on some of our closest-held beliefs.

Now that's not good enough. We're currently experiencing the intolerance of intolerance (hopefully you catch the hypocrisy in that). Christians with "traditional" convictions and understandings of sexuality and marriage are seen as "bigots"—churches are being viewed as "hate groups." Our beliefs are, Bernie says and millions of others think, "hateful." Our positions are, Bernie says and millions of others think, "backwards."

Welcome to the age of unbelief. What are we going to do in it?

I believe we can thrive.

Really.

WE WILL RESPOND — BUT HOW?

As we live in this cultural moment as Christians, each of us responds in one way or another. We have to. We may do it with great thought, or we may do it based on gut instinct or on what everyone else at our church is doing—but we will respond. And I think that response will take one of four basic approaches. I want to lay them out for you, and I want to say first up that none are altogether wrong, but that the first three—two of which I'm borrowing as concepts from Andy Crouch's book *Culture Making*—are problematic.

So first, we can take what might be called the *converting culture* approach.

In this mindset, what matters most is that our nation's culture reflects biblical principles and values. Supporters of this view are willing to go to great lengths to make it happen, even if that means making alliances with corrupted politicians and political parties, or making what they might see as lesser moral compromises. Think the "Christian Right," especially as of late.

But in a span of history where the church doesn't have high cultural standing, this approach is going to leave a lot of people frustrated and bitter. It already has. It will only perpetuate what has been known as "the culture wars," a frankly arrogant posture that pits the church against the world, and does not draw a healthy line between the kingdom of God now and the kingdom of God to come.

I'm not going to pretend that there aren't some good aspects of "converting culture." You can trace much of its roots to the work of amazing theologians like Abraham Kuyper and Francis Schaeffer. It recognizes the reality that

Christians should be engaged in all of culture, seeking to transform culture through the power of Christ, through whom all things were created and through whom all things are sustained. After all, Christ is not just the Lord of the church, but of the world.

And yes, Christians are called to seek the good of those around us, and to pursue justice and to love good and shun evil. But we get into trouble when we confuse the earthly city with the heavenly city. Until Christ returns, this world will never look as it should. You can't use politics to build the new Jerusalem, and you can't legislate people into the kingdom of God.

In fact, I'd argue that the compromises and unholy alliances Christians have made in pursuit of converting the culture have left many people more suspicious of and hardened to the message of the church. And I don't blame them.

Where do we go, then? Well, the next option is to respond to the age of unbelief by what I call *condemning culture*. This is the idea of removing ourselves from the world, retreating into a subculture, and staying well away from wider culture because society is sinful, corrupted and antithetical to the gospel of Jesus Christ.

This stream has always been part of the church's response to the challenge of living in this world. You see it in the rise of the monasteries. You see it in various parts of the Anabaptist movement. You see it today in blogs and books advising Christians to create their own sub-culture, withdrawing from the increasingly un-Christian and, yes, anti-Christian wider culture. There's certainly something admirable and beautiful in this. God does call his people to holiness. The Scriptures are clear about the church being distinct from the rest of the world. We are to be salt—we are to "taste" different.

My concern is that, by itself, I just don't think the idea is all that biblical. We are to be "the salt of the earth" (Matthew 5 v 13)—and salt maintains its flavor while it is rubbed into the foodstuff it is being used to preserve.

Not only that: salt spreads its flavor too. There comes a point where we have to actually get our hands dirty and show and share the good news of Christ, and proximity and relationships are essential to making that work. It requires involvement in the local community and in the "public square." If God's Old Testament people could be called to "seek the welfare of the city" of Babylon during their exile from their homeland (Jeremiah 29 v 7), then we should be seeking the welfare of ours, too.

After all, however ungodly your context, you're not in Babylon.

The truth is that whether we're talking food, technology, music or other entertainment, God gives us these things as good gifts to be enjoyed, as long as we keep them in their right place by not elevating creation over the Creator. We can be skeptical of them, but we shouldn't be fearful of them. Culture is not the source of evil. That's the human heart (Mark 7 v 18-23)—and so closing out the culture won't close out sin.

The third popular response to post-Christian culture is in many ways the most attractive, the most widespread, and the most scary. It's to follow the trends—to *consume culture.* So wherever culture and historical Christian teaching disagree, the latter is accommodated to the former. After all, if we want to stay relevant in a post-Christian age, then some of the Christian stuff will have to go, right?

In most cases, those who take this approach start in a good place, with good intentions of seeing where the Bible speaks boldly and clearly about social issues that we often ignore, and embracing the connection between faith and culture. As the Manhattan-based pastor Tim Keller said in his critique of this position in his book *Center Church*:

"This model sees Christianity as being fundamentally compatible with the surrounding culture. Those who embrace this model believe that God is at work redemptively within cultural movements that have nothing explicitly to do with Christianity."

But the problem comes when we start to put too great a focus on culture to the neglect of the gospel, and that even goes for social justice. What happens is that we start to want the implications of the gospel more than we want the actual gospel.

Those who take the "consuming culture" approach follow culture, first and foremost, before the Bible, neglecting and compromising on significant aspects of faith. These men and women begin to look more and more like the world and less and less like the church. When the voice of a culture, and not the word of Christ, is what governs the church, then it is no longer the church. It's just a social club of people desperately trying to keep up with the cultural fashion. Ironically, that's the quickest way to close your church. Why would anyone bother coming to a church that is indistinguishable from anything else?!

These three options—*converting, condemning, and consuming*—are all very different, but I think they all have something in common. They are born of fear.

Those in the "converting culture" camp fear they are losing their culture and that if they do not make the compromises necessary to continue the culture war, the church cannot thrive, or even survive.

Those in the "condemning culture" camp fear that culture will corrupt them and the church; that any connection will lead to contamination and the church will become sick.

Those in the "consuming culture" camp fear that the church will become unacceptable and therefore irrelevant to those who are steeped in post-Christian culture, and that if the church is to have a future it must get with the program.

WHAT WE NEED

You may have guessed by now that this book will not encourage you to convert, condemn or consume the culture. I want to give you something else: a fourth option.

And I don't want to offer you a strategy so much as a posture. I want to address the fears that grip our hearts and that drive so much of our responses as Christians to the age of unbelief.

I want to give you courage.

I want to give you a posture that allows you to look round and think, *This is a great time to be a Christian.*

That's what Christians most need in a post-9/11, post-Christian, post-modern, post-everything world. If our hearts are not in the right place, if our hopes are misaligned, anything we try to do will be shortlived and misguided.

So this book is about where to find real courage and how to live by it. I'm convinced that if we have a God-sized, God-given courage, then we will be freed up to be the people of God, living out the mission of God, marked by the joy of God.

With courage, this season of history can be viewed not with fear and trepidation, but instead with hope and a sense of opportunity.

With courage, our perspectives change, and we can be excited and encouraged about this cultural moment, and not intimidated, angered, or paralyzed by it.

Welcome to the age of unbelief. The church can thrive here.

All we need is Christian courage.

Take heart.

2. WHERE WE ARE AND HOW WE GOT HERE

We're in the age of unbelief because we are in the twilight of Christendom. And that's a good thing.

We are leaving behind what might be the most unusual period of human history for God's people. If you consider the people of God throughout the history of humanity and around the world, we've rarely been at the center of cultural and political power. Our forefathers in the faith were almost always at the margins of society. In fact, the very roots of the church grew from the soil of a Roman Empire that attempted to stamp out the faith, feeding early Christians to lions, putting them in prison, crucifying them upside down, and boiling them alive.

If you told a second-century version of yourself, *Hey, in 500 years or so, our senior pastors will be living in palaces, our church leaders will be exempt from taxes and the law, and* everyone around here will call themselves a Christian because, well, it's just what you do, they'd assume you'd gone mad. When we look at the people of God throughout the Old Testament and the New Testament and in the centuries that followed, Christians always found themselves on the margins of society.

Then everything changed.

To do a little history here: in the first half of the fourth century, an about-to-be Roman emperor named Constantine converted to Christianity, just before gaining power over the western half of the Roman Empire (later, he would add the eastern half to his property portfolio). The first Roman emperor to pledge his allegiance to Christ and call Jesus "Lord," Constantine helped implement an agreement for Christians to be treated benevolently within the empire.

By the late fourth century, Christianity had become the official religion of the Roman Empire. Before you knew it, bishops were suddenly giving advice to the emperor instead of being fed to lions by the emperor. For better or worse, the fourth century witnessed the marriage of the Christian church and the Roman state. Christendom had officially dawned.

Over the next few centuries, the Christian faith spread even further outside the rule and reign of the Roman Empire. It came to include the whole of Europe, Russia, and then eventually America. And everywhere—even where, toward the end of the age, there was a technical separation of church and state—it was the state religion. What came to be known as the "Western world" was essentially Christendom.

HOW CHRISTENDOM CHANGED THE CHURCH

I don't know if you paid attention in history class (or if they even mentioned Christendom in your class), but not all of Christendom was merry and bright. In spite of what might appear to be a wonderful movement of the Spirit, in which over half of the world professed faith in Christ (and I'm not denying that God used this span of history to grow his church), there has always been a gross underbelly to it all.

In his book *Post-Christendom: Church and Mission in a Strange New World*, Stuart Murray helps us understand Christendom a bit better—both the good and the ill. I want to highlight four of the hallmarks that he examines from this era.

First, as Christendom formed, you began to get what was considered to be a "Christian civilization." The world was broken into categories. There was Christendom, and then there were the heathens or barbarians. This divide became based around geographical locations. You were a Christian by virtue of being born in a Christian country. So in 1400, if you were born in France, you were a Christian. If you were born in China, you were not. That was it.

Second, the church moved from the margins and became the center of political and cultural power. The people of God, who had spent most of history as outsiders, as the persecuted, oppressed and exiled, now enjoyed the power and prestige of being on the inside. The leaders of the church enjoyed huge influence and amassed great wealth. They decided the ethics of a society and directed the political temperature of a given state.

Where there once had been a great divide between church and state, there was now a close-knit marriage.

Third, Sunday became an official day of rest, and churchgoing was at the very least socially mandatory. In most cases, I'm not talking about police officers kicking open your door and arresting you if you weren't at Sunday school—though that's basically what would have happened in late-sixteenth-century England if you didn't turn up to your local Anglican church often enough. I'm saying there were cultural ramifications for not belonging to a church.

This was certainly true in mid-late twentieth-century America. Back then if you were a smart and successful businessman, you were a member of the First Baptist Church or the First Methodist Church or whatever. If you wanted to be respected in your community, you needed to belong to a church. If you didn't, you might belong to the heathens, and folks were wary of letting you fix their car or sell them groceries.

Fourth, Christendom changed the way churches worked. There came a divide between what we can call the "laity" (ordinary Christians) and the "clergy" (the professional ministers)—a divide that even the best efforts of the Reformers in the 1500s and 1600s did not roll back. The church gradually became an institution with professionals paid to do the church stuff, and everyone else's job was just to show up.

We are totally desensitized to this division today, but this setup just didn't exist in the early church. Before this shift, there was a missionary force proclaiming and heralding the gospel and making disciples in one of the most world-changing movements this earth has ever seen. The historian Rodney Stark estimates that by AD 350, just before Christendom really became a thing, 51 percent of those living in the Roman Empire claimed Christ as King, despite the social exclusion and physical danger such loyalty brought with it.

That statistic is remarkable, and it's no coincidence that such growth came at a time of immense persecution. But the truth is that in general (and there are exceptions, but this is the basic rule), the more a government tries to subject and destroy Christianity, the more it flourishes. The more it is given friendly quarter, the more it grows weak and stale and soft—professional, rather than missional.

THE CRACKS APPEAR

While there were certainly times of struggle and decay, Christendom reigned supreme for roughly 1,400 years throughout Europe and the Americas until cracks began to form in its might. These cracks were caused primarily by the Enlightenment.

The "Enlightenment" wasn't a particular event, but more of a movement among the intellectual elites that began in the 18th century. It was a period when a whole bunch of philosophers and thinkers across Europe started challenging received wisdom and discussing new ideas about politics, society, and religion.

Ironically, given its name, it was the Enlightenment that began to turn down the lights on Christendom. That's because (and here's a summary of this movement in about three paragraphs—it's not going to be full and nuanced) Enlightenment thinkers considered mankind as, to borrow James K.A. Smith's phrase, "brains on a stick." That means that human reason—and the intellect—is king. It's the idea that what you observe is all there is, and what you reason out is what is right. There's nothing that's supernatural. If you can't taste it or see it or touch it or hear it or smell it, it doesn't exist, or at least it doesn't count when it comes to working out how to live.

Though many Enlightenment thinkers still believed in God, this line of thinking led to a way of life where

God ceased to be the center of reality—man became the center. The famous phrase of the seventeenth-century philosopher René Descartes, "I think; therefore I am," served as a kind of bumper-sticker slogan for the Enlightenment—my sense of what is true, good, and beautiful begins and usually ends with my brain, my reason, myself. The solution of all mankind's ills can be found in the mind of man, as the mind of man fixes what's wrong. Reason trumps belief.

Enlightenment thinking brought some great advances in religious liberty, human rights, and tolerance. We take these things for granted today, but we should remain grateful for these legacies of that movement. These are things the church should have spoken out on (and should still speak out on today), but sadly it took the Enlightenment to do it.

One other consequence of Enlightenment thinking was the beginning of the dusk of Christendom. Before long, the church was no longer considered to be the guardian of moral and ethical behavior. For the first time in 1,400 years, some of the cultural influencers began to say, *The church doesn't get to decide what's right and wrong. We will use our brains to work out for ourselves what is right and what is wrong.*

That's a massive shift, and we're beginning to feel the full weight of it today—in this age of unbelief.

THE CHURCH AND ME

Given its emphasis on man as the center of life, the Enlightenment was the source of modern-day individualism, materialism, and consumerism. Each of these not only led people away from the church, but they have also greatly influenced the church—both in the way people understand it and the way it operates.

Basically, we began to see church from a consumerist viewpoint, as a place that existed to help us, to serve us, and to meet our needs—not as a place in which to be the body of Christ and to worship God. So rather than the church being something we give our lives to, it became another option on the great and ever-growing menu of life and leisure choices. Maybe we do it. Maybe we don't. Devotion to the gathering of God's people and the worship of God's name became an add-on to the rest of life.

Sure, no one would actually say this, but we often tend to think this way: *We're not doing anything this Saturday and, man, that church has services on Saturday. Here's what we could do, baby. We could just drop the kids off and hang out. The music there is good. That guy who does the preaching sometimes is funny. He might go off on a rant, but we can just turn him off and look at our phones. It's like a little date night for us. And it's free.*

And unfortunately churches have fed into this consumerist, individualistic model of faith. Sermon series and books seem to be less about the character and nature of God and, well, the actual Bible, and more about ways that we can improve or better our lives. There's been a shift from orienting our lives around God and his story to orienting God around our life stories. It's what Christian Smith dubbed "moralistic-therapeutic-deism." It's a religion of trying to be good people so that we can feel good about ourselves; and God's name is mentioned here and there, but he's really somewhere in the distance.

What ends up happening is that a local church enters a competitive marketplace against other churches. Rather than being on mission and longing to see people come to know Christ, we just reshuffle the deck of Christians in a given city. Then things just get out of hand, and our churches start to look more and more like the world and less and less like Christ. It's getting to the point where you show up, push a button on your chair and someone brings you a mocha to drink. Then at the end of the performance—because that's what it is—you basically just pick your kids up at Main Event and head home again. I'm exaggerating, of course—but not much.

FROM THE CENTER TO THE MARGINS

But that's all passing. Now we find ourselves in a society where not only fewer people are confessing Christ as Lord, but more people are beginning to grow hostile toward him, and his people. In that context, no impressive smoke machine or great kids' entertainment is going to keep people coming to a gathering which seems not just out of touch, but outdated and foolish.

The church has been removed from its place of cultural and political power, and is being pushed further and further toward the margins. Europe has already felt this shift for several decades, and we're now feeling it in full force here throughout the United States.

Make no mistake, whether you like it or not, the margins are where we're headed.

In many ways, we're already there.

One illustration of how radical and how fast this thing has moved is Truett Cathy and his son Dan Cathy, who are respectively the founder and the current CEO of the fast-food chain Chick-fil-A. These are men who love Jesus Christ. They give away millions and millions and millions of dollars to all sorts of needs all over the world.

In an interview with a Christian publication, Dan Cathy was asked a question about his business model, and he responded with the following:

"We are very much supportive of the family, the biblical definition of the family unit. We are a family-owned business, a family-led business, and we are married to our first wives. We give God thanks for that. We know it might not be popular with everyone, but thank the Lord we live in a country where we can share our values and operate on biblical principles."

Soon, Dan's interview spread around the rest of the media, leading to outrage. And in a follow-up interview (words of wisdom, by the way: never do a follow-up interview) he was asked about his views on marriage. He said:

"I think we are inviting God's judgment on our nation when we shake our fist at him and say, 'We know better than you as to what constitutes a marriage.' I pray God's mercy on our generation that has such a prideful, arrogant attitude to think that we have the audacity to define what marriage is all about."

Now any sensible, reasonable person can read Dan's answer and agree or disagree, but they can't accuse him of hate or bigotry. That's simply not the case. But that's not how a good portion of the world responded.

Despite the fact that you don't have to be a Christian to work for Chick-fil-A, and despite the fact that you don't have to have any particular sexual orientation or preference, and despite the fact that research shows it's a place that equally loves and serves all people, the whole of Chick-fil-A began to be viewed as a sort of hate establishment.

Social media got fired up.

There were protests.

Practically every major news publication ran an editorial article that leaned heavily against the restaurant franchise.

Then the politicians waded in.

Rahm Emanuel, the mayor of Chicago, said, "Chick-fil-A values are not Chicago values."

James Kenney is a Philadelphia councilman, and he called Dan's comment "hate speech."

Boston's mayor, Thomas Menino, vowed to block any attempts to open a Chick-fil-A in Boston.

Chicago alderman Joe Moreno said he would deny Chick-fil-A a permit if they tried to open a restaurant in his neighborhood.

San Francisco's mayor, Ed Lee, said he recommended that Chick-fil-A not try to come closer than a 40-mile distance from San Francisco—which sounds as reasonable as one kid threatening to beat up another kid in high school.

Ten years ago in the United States, this whole situation wouldn't have been news. But the climate has changed. The culture has changed. The church once again is being pushed into the margins, and that's very uncomfortable for us.

Yet I'm not mourning the death of Christendom.

I welcome it.

Here's why.

THRIVING BEYOND THE MIRAGE

First, the church thrives on the margins. That's why our cultural moment doesn't need to be viewed as depressing but, instead, exciting. It's not bad news. It's good news. We're now back in the place where we have always flourished best.

Second, it gives us the perspective required to see that Christendom was essentially a mirage. There's no such thing as a Christian America—or any other Christian nation for that matter.

Now I do believe our country was founded by mostly Christian men and upon a number of core Christian beliefs. And, for a good portion of our nation's history, many held close to these founding principles. You can't really argue with that. Because I believe the Creator of this universe knows the best way for his creation to operate, I also think our faith provides the best framework for our country—and any country for that matter.

But it's hard to look at the history of the United States— just as it's hard to look at any part of Christendom—and make a case for it being "Christian." Sure, we can look at how everyone used to claim to be a Christian and went to church every Sunday—the whole "God and country" idea. But then you have to do something with the attempted genocide of the Native American people, with slavery, with Jim Crow racial segregation laws... and the list goes on.

This is one reason I think a show like *Mad Men* is so helpful and enlightening. Centered on an advertising agency in the 1960s, specifically its sleazy yet brilliant creative director, Don Draper, *Mad Men* turns the American dream on its head. The show portrays this time and place as no better than the world in which we live today—if not more horrendous, especially given the presence of racism and sexism.

The men cheat on their wives.

They cheat at their jobs.

They do whatever it takes to get ahead and fulfill their lustful desires.

The women don't behave any better. They, too, cheat to get ahead.

They throw themselves at men.

They disregard their kids.

They gossip among their friends.

Mad Men de-romanticizes our wistful view of an era that was supposedly "Christian."

I love my country and count it a blessing from the Lord to have been raised here and to get to raise a family here. But I don't think we can be both honest and say it was (far less is) somehow a "Christian nation." The end of Christendom enables us to see it for what it always was—no more or less sinful than this new age of unbelief.

Then third, I don't mourn the passing of Christendom because I think a lot of people claim to be Christians who aren't Christians. They're "Christians" because they were born in Texas, or their parents went to church, or they walked forward at an altar call, or they got baptized. They haven't submitted their life to the rule of Jesus Christ, but for them that's not what it's about. They're Christians because it's a club, and they may be a non-playing member but they're still a member, and so God will bless them and God will welcome them into heaven, right?

This is called nominalism, and nominalism is a weed that grows so fast and roots so deep in the soil of Christendom.

And I think the death of this strange era will solve that. Marginalization will help people realize, *No, I don't really care for Jesus. I just thought church was fun. It was just a hobby of mine. Christ didn't have my heart. I had just found a place where I could play volleyball with some friends.*

Marginalization is the space where we find out where our loves and our allegiances really lie.

That's because, in this era, we are going to need to get used to no longer being seen as honorable, but to being seen as bigots. We are going to have to realize that, in our workplaces and in our sports clubs and, well, pretty much everywhere, people will respond to our views on life and death and marriage and sex in the same way they did with Dan Cathy at Chick-fil-A—with outrage, ridicule, and even aggression.

We are going to have to accept that Christendom is dying, that in many places in this nation (as throughout the

West) it's already dead, and that that's both a hard thing and a good thing.

HOW TO FIND OUT THAT YOU'RE BRAVE

This is how we got to where we are today, and why I don't mourn that we are where we are today. But living faithfully and effectively as God's people in the age of unbelief won't happen automatically or accidentally.

We are going to need to live with courage.

And that's easier said than it is done. After all, it's hard to be brave in the dark. But then again, it's only in the dark that you can find out that you're brave. Anyone can play the tough guy when it's light.

But what I want you to be, and what I want our churches to be, is courageous. The church before Christendom was made up of individuals who had a courage that could not be quenched by the fires nor torn apart by the lions. It was made up of ordinary people who together unleashed an unstoppable multiplication of churches through the known world.

The church after Christendom can, by God's grace, rediscover that courage and rediscover that mission. And it starts with you and me; and our response to the twilight of Christendom can be and must be to step out in courage instead of fear—not a courage that we muster up and maintain by our strength and our efforts, but a courage that comes from the Lord and that causes us to continue to call on the Lord.

3. THE GOD WE LOOK TO

Courage is something that it's far easier to talk about than to live out of. It's always easier live out of fear of one kind or another.

But fear never changed anything for the better. Fear never kept the church standing firm. Fear never produced joy. Fear won't free us to live positively and confidently and Christianly on the margins.

So we need to junk our fears and just replace them with courage, right?

Wrong.

Under the pseudonym Ambrose Redoom, the writer James Neil Hollingworth once wrote:

"Courage is not the absence of fear, but rather the judgment that something else is more important than one's fear."

That's so helpful. We tend to think courage is the lack of fear, but that's just not true. If there's no fear, there can't be courage. You must feel fear to be courageous.

Real courage takes place when you are anxious, when you are worried, when you just don't know how to push through—but then there's something more valuable, something greater than that fear. So though you feel fear, your actions are not driven by that fear. They are directed by something else. You step out with courage because there is something else that drives you—something that is greater than what you're afraid of.

Historically, when the culture seemed to be behind the church in the era of Christendom, we were part of the so-called "moral majority." We stood boldly and firmly, always assuming that the culture had our backs. We could say, *This is a really bad thing,* and 90 percent of the culture would go, *Yeah, you're right. It is a bad thing.* In many ways, those days required little courage.

And those days are long gone.

We are no longer a moral majority. Given this sweeping societal shift, many will cave in to the culture at some point because they're afraid of being seen as irrelevant or not being worthy of respect—they'll consume culture.

Many will become angry and frustrated, and spend their waking hours trying to get us back to Christendom—they'll be aiming at converting culture.

Many will avoid the culture altogether, creating subcultures, and do their own thing when it comes to art, education, commerce and politics, condemning culture.

As I said, at some level all these responses are motivated by fear. But if we're directed by courage, we'll walk forward positively, faithfully, and joyfully.

Where do we find that kind of courage? What will be the basis of our courage when we are not seen as the sane ones, not seen as the compassionate ones, not seen as loving or gracious, because our culture has decided that to disagree is to hate?

We need to know God.

MORE THAN CONQUERORS

Let me take you from post-Christendom to pre-Christendom, and to the words of Paul.

If you're ever feeling inadequate or insufficient because of your failures and weaknesses, it's always helpful to remember Paul. He was a man who had hated Christ and hated Christians, who had set his face to destroy them, who was, according to his own biography, a murderer, a torturer, and a violent blasphemer—and yet who became one of the greatest missionaries the Christian faith has ever known. God isn't looking for polished, perfect people. He's always worked through people who know that they are sinners and who are amazed that they have been saved.

Paul's letter to the Romans was addressed to a church long before the rulers of the Roman Empire shifted in favor of the Christian faith. These were believers living in a period when persecution was beginning to rise and when, in the not-too-distant future, Christians would be burned alive and fed to lions. That's the audience of the epistle. And I'm not saying that things will get this bad again for the church in the West (I sure hope not). But as we move more and more toward a society where Christianity seems to have no place, especially in the public square, the context of these early believers being mocked and mistreated for their faith resonates with us more and more.

Paul spoke both realistically and boldly to these men and women:

"For [God's] sake we are being killed all the day long; we are regarded as sheep to be slaughtered. [But] in all these things we are more than conquerors through him who loved us."
(Romans 8 v 36-37)

I can't reiterate enough the significance of reading these words through the eyes of Christians whose stuff was being stolen simply because of their faith, whose career prospects were diminishing fast simply because of their faith, and for whom imprisonment was a very realistic possibility simply because of their faith.

We need to understand the temptation they must have felt to consume, convert, or condemn the culture of the time.

But Paul wanted them to live with courage instead—with the courage of knowing that they were "more than conquerors," because they were infinitely and unstoppably loved by the God whom Paul goes on to describe in Romans 11 v 33-36:

"Oh, the depth of the riches and wisdom and knowledge of God! How unsearchable are his judgments and how inscrutable his ways! 'For who has known the mind of the Lord, or who has been his counselor?' 'Or who has given a gift to him that he might be repaid?' For from him and through him and to him are all things. To him be glory forever. Amen."

As children of the Enlightenment and as sinners prone to focus inwardly instead of upwardly, we tend to look for confidence within ourselves. That's why it's important to see what Paul is doing here. He is pleading with us to get our eyes off ourselves and on God.

That's how you get courage.

You look at God.

GOD'S RICHES ARE DEEP

Paul starts by talking about God's riches. At first, that seems like a random thing to bring up. But when we think about the fact that his original audience was living in a society where their belongings were being stolen and where their possessions were being taken away, it makes a lot more sense.

Most of us can relate to this. We all know the immense stress that comes with finances—and for most of us, that's just us trying to live within our means and balance our budgets. But right now, in the US and the UK, there are Christian business owners (or ex-business owners) who already are literally counting the cost of holding faithfully to Christ. Thinking about our riches or lack of them will conquer us with fear. Paul says, *Let's talk about God's riches.*

You see, as human beings made in the image of God, we can only create what we can afford, out of what actually exists and which we have access to. Recently, my wife remodeled our house. She was constrained in this remodeling project by two things.

The first was finances—what we could actually afford.

The second was raw material. She needed two-by-fours. She needed sheetrock. I think that there was also some sort of weird metal that existed only in one place on earth that was shipped in from some far-off country to serve as a light switch or something.

We're constrained in what we can build by what we have resources for. But that's not how God works.

The creation narrative in Genesis 1 – 2 is not a story about how God lived in heaven and out of necessity, with heaven being so packed, needed a place to put all that stuff—so he threw it out into the universe. No, there was nothing until God told there to be something. That's awesome. God just said, "Let there be... let us make..." (Genesis 1 v 3, 6, 14, 26), and the word that spoke everything into being was so powerful that the universe continues to expand in every direction to this day.

I don't know how you're rolling. I don't know what kind of bank balance you have, but I do know that you cannot do that. Let me prove it to you:

Build a boat, right now.

You can't.

Or at least, you can't do it instantly. (And you knew that.) You're constrained. It's only God who doesn't need anything, and can just speak as much as he wants or anything he wants into existence without any raw material. He just tells it to be, and he has it. That's a kind of wealth that you and I cannot comprehend. But it is a wealth that belongs to the triune God, and that means that it is part of what Paul is talking about. God the Father, through his Son and by his Spirit, is going to share all his riches with his children.

Paul encourages us to avoid putting our heads down to keep our money safe and our possessions intact. He reminds us that it doesn't matter what is taken from us. It doesn't ultimately matter if we end up being broke or in prison. The wealth of God is immense and eternally ours. Appreciating our Father's richness gives us courage that conquers our fears of what we may lose in the here and now.

GOD'S WISDOM IS LONG

Paul goes on to put our eyes on the wisdom and knowledge of God. He wants those Christians in Rome to consider the truth that God knows what is coming because God has planned what is coming. He wants them to consider what things could look like in 10,000 years.

Remember who Paul is writing to—believers in Rome. They would not have been able to fathom the end of the Roman Empire. Their houses were in what was known as the Eternal City. Rome stood at the pinnacle of its might in this period—and Paul's readers would not have been able to imagine that ever changing. It was just how the world was at the time. It was the lens through which everyone saw life.

And yet, just a few years ago, I spent 12 euros to walk through Rome's ruins. Now there is no Roman Empire—except in the history books.

The point is that God, who sees all and knows all, is managing things in ways we can't comprehend. He's playing the long game, and we need to hear that because we live in a culture that doesn't value the long game. Our digital, throwaway culture of instant information and instant gratification struggles to see the big picture. We want everything, and we want it quickly. But that's not how the Lord works. The Lord will not become a slave to our cultural assumptions or demands.

He's just too big for that.

This is important because there will come a day when you will be marginalized, ridiculed, or oppressed for your faith, if it hasn't already happened. In that moment, the wisdom and knowledge of the Father will be of massive importance to you. When we begin to enter these spaces, whether it involves losing friends, struggling to find a job, or actually ending up in prison for being a Christian, there will be a temptation to lose hope and lose trust. But Paul tells us, *No, no, no. In all things, God knows what he's doing.*

Because we are finite beings, we find ourselves in a given location and in a given time. I am writing in Dallas, Texas, in the second decade of the twenty-first century since Christ walked the earth. That's where I am and when I am. This time and place includes its own cultural particularities. It contains its own feel and vibe. It's my context. It colors the way I see the world.

That is not how the triune God of the Bible works. God is not inside time; he is outside of time, so he sees it all in a way that's seamless and doesn't register with us.

This idea might blow your mind, but the future is not a time that God knows about: *it's a place where he is.* He is all there in the way that he is all here in the way that he is all in the farthest reaches of the universe. God is outside of time; and in being outside of time, his wisdom and knowledge are inscrutable. They can't be questioned because we don't even have the intellectual capacity to ask the right questions!

Saint Augustine, the fourth-century bishop of Hippo, said that to be human is to have your face pushed up against a stained-glass window. You see some color, but you see a lot of glass fragments. It is only given to God and those who are with him to be back far enough to see the whole window.

To put it differently, to tell God the Father that he should do things differently is to step into a three-hour-long movie for two seconds, and then step back out and lecture the director on the storyline. That's what it's like. You just don't know, and he—the fountain of life—does.

Romans 8 and Romans 11 remind us that God knows. To Christians experiencing persecution and marginalization, Paul is saying, *God has not abandoned you. He has not forgotten you. Whatever your two-second perspective tells you, you have to remember that he has a depth and length of wisdom and knowledge that you can't even start to comprehend.*

And we can see from history, as well as know from Scripture, how right that is. Within three hundred years, more than half of the empire's population would claim to be Christians. Within 2,000 years, a guy like me would be paying pocket change to marvel at the remains of the jail cells in which those apparently all-powerful Roman authorities put my spiritual ancestors.

We may feel anxious as we head into the age of unbelief. Who knows how long it will last, how hard it will be, or what will come next.

Well, God does, actually.

We know that God is sovereign and infinitely wise and knowing, and we can take heart in remembering and believing that he's got this thing—that our small slice of history is just that, a small slice, and God has got a bigger, greater plan in place that will not be stopped or hindered. As Jesus, the Son, tells Peter in Matthew 16, even the gates of hell will not prevail against his church.

THINK YOURSELF SMALL

God is unspeakably rich. He's infinitely knowledgeable. And that leads Paul to do what really is the unforgivable sin in our current cultural context. *He says you should think less of yourself.*

You should feel lower and smaller and weaker than you naturally do. It likely sounds counter-intuitive, in a season of difficulty, to embrace feeling weaker and smaller. But in God's economy, to lack confidence in yourself is the first and necessary stage in gaining confidence in God.

That's where I think the church has made such a big mistake in these last hundred years or so. We've spent years telling each other, *You can do it. You're so great. Be yourself. Find yourself. Believe in yourself.* Our teaching and advice has been based more on the false wisdom of our world than the true wisdom of the word. And that means we've ended up trying to run a marathon on cotton candy. We've tried to be bold in the day of war while eating Twinkies.

We have a vacuum where we should have a big view of God.

To live with real courage requires us to live with a right assessment of our own weakness. It requires us to measure ourselves against the Lord and realize we are very, very small. That's what Paul gets us to do in verse 34:

> *"'For who has known the mind of the Lord, or who has been his counselor?' 'Or who has given a gift to him that he might be repaid?'"*

There's no one who can answer this. When this epistle was read aloud to the church in Rome, and they reached this part of the letter, there was no one who stopped the reader and said, *Oh, wait, I know the mind of the Lord!* and then got interrupted by someone at the back calling out, *Hang on, I actually did give a gift to God—he does owe me!*

No—I would bet there was silence.

No one on this earth knows enough to understand the ways of God or to counsel God. He needs none of us and he owes none of us. God doesn't owe you anything. You have nothing to give to him that is not already his.

It's the equivalent of my young children buying me birthday presents. I will not be a wealthier man when I receive those gifts—because those gifts will be bought with money I earned. My kids will go to their mother and ask their mother for money to buy me a present, and my wife will give them money from our joint account to buy me presents. My heart will be full that they thought of me, and it's so sweet, but

I'm going to have a hole in my bank account that is exactly the value of those gifts. I won't owe them, since they just gave me what was already mine.

It's the same way with God. He is no man's debtor.

C.S. Lewis's *Mere Christianity* makes the point this way: to try to give anything to God is like getting sixpence from your grandfather and buying him a gift and bringing it back to him. The grandfather is sixpence none the richer (that's where the "Kiss Me" band Sixpence None the Richer got their name from).

Everything you have has been given to you by God for the glory of God. You cannot now leverage it to put God in your debt. Whenever you feel that welling up in you—that feeling that you deserve better—well, that's based on the view that you've somehow made God owe you, but God doesn't owe you anything, which makes everything good in your life a cause to worship.

He is no man's debtor. It's all a gift from him. Every breath is a present, every laugh a grace, every smile a mercy.

God does not need you, and God does not owe you. He's much, much, infinitely bigger and greater than that. And, when we get a glimpse of this God, all we can and should do is realize how small we are and how great he is, and echo what Paul says:

"From him and through him and to him are all things. To him be glory forever. Amen." (v 36)

OUR GOD IS ABLE

When we begin to get a handle on the greatness of God, we begin to get a great, God-given, God-sized courage.

When we take our eyes off ourselves and look up to the glory, wisdom and riches of God, we are given strength and hope.

In other words, when we look to God, we get courage to live for God. We get the kind of courage that brings us peace, joy, and positivity when we are under pressure.

As the Civil Rights action started to really heat up and people actually started to get seriously beaten and even killed, and there were a lot of threats going around, Martin Luther King, Jr. wrote a sermon called *Our God is Able*, that turned into a paper, that turned into part of a book called *Strength to Love*. Amid hostility and violence, Dr. King said:

"It seemed as though I heard an inner voice saying, 'Stand up for righteousness. Stand up for truth. God will be at your side forever.' Almost at once my fears began to pass from me. The outer situation remained the same, but God had given me inner calm.

"Three nights later [while Dr. King was out of town], our home was bombed. Strangely enough, I accepted the word of the bombing calmly ... My experience with God had given me new strength and trust... I know now that God is able to give us the interior resources to face the storms of life."

What Dr. King describes is a supernatural act. You don't find that courage from looking deep within yourself. It doesn't come from being mad at the world or from keeping your head down in the world.

It comes from experiencing God.

Dr. King met the God of glory in his word and in prayer, and the same God who gave him "new strength and trust" is the same God who gives us strength and trust today. Our God does not always make the storms of opposition go away, but he is always able to make us stand up for righteousness and truth in those storms. That's the God-given courage that comes from having a view of the greatness of the God who is at our sides.

A FEAR THAT DOESN'T LAST

When I look at the cultural landscape—the political situation, the economic situation, the racial divide, global terrorism, the numbers leaving the church, the growing hostility toward God's word—I begin to feel afraid. I get that impulse.

But we can't sit in this fear.

We can't let this fear grip us and cripple us, robbing us of our joy and holding us back from living faithfully and holding out the gospel.

It's okay to feel fear. That's normal. That's human. We're weak and frail.

But we must not stay in that place. We must move beyond it. We must learn to lean on something bigger; we must find something greater that transcends it—or rather, we must learn to lean on Someone greater.

The courage we need only comes from getting our eyes off of ourselves, and onto the Lord. That is not an idea that will get quoted alongside a cute picture of your coffee cup and Bible on Instagram. But it's so freeing and so transformational. God is far greater, far more eternal, far more sovereign, far more wonderful than anything this world may take from you.

We are more than conquerors, always, through him who loves us.

4. THE STORY WE LIVE IN

A.W. Tozer was one of the greatest theologians of the twentieth century. In a book called *The Knowledge of the Holy,* he once wrote,

"What comes into our minds when we think about God is the most important thing about us."

When you think about God, what you think about him will shape everything about you. It will shape how you approach marriage, money, work, leisure, parenting and so on. It will literally shape everything you do.

So when you think about God, if you think he is gracious and kind and loving and forgiving, then your relationships will be defined by grace, you'll tend to give people the benefit of the doubt, and you'll handle your resources generously.

If, on the other hand, you think of God as being perpetually disappointed in you, like your performance gets you into and out of his favor, then you'll likely treat others with anger or anxiety, and approach life with a type of greediness that shows you are trying to buy or to earn a peace that ultimately is not earnable.

What we think of when we think about God matters. That's why it's so pivotal that we recover an attribute of God that is so easily ignored or dismissed for various reasons.

Some find it strange.

Some find it scary.

Some totally miss the point of it.

Yet it's an attribute that, when we know it, consider it, and believe it, will give us courage in this age of unbelief: it's the understanding that *God is a warrior.*

This attribute of God has almost completely vanished today—when did you last hear a sermon on the warrior nature of our God? When we think about God, we tend to think about Nickelodeon, not HBO—about Disney, not *Dunkirk.*

Without realizing it, we can end up with a Tinker Bell Jesus, who has a bag of pixie dust and all he does is sprinkle us with blessings. He never gets upset about anything. You can't do anything wrong. His sprinkle dust is there to help you understand that, yes, you really are amazing.

Don't get me wrong. You cannot think too much about or appreciate too deeply the grace, mercy, long-suffering, patience and kindness of the triune God. We must never neglect those attributes of God. God is not only a warrior, and this is only one way of thinking and speaking about him. Of course he's more than a warrior; but he's not less. Make no mistake, the Bible does paint God as a warrior.

"The LORD is a man of war; the LORD is his name."
(Exodus 15 v 3)

Yet that might not mean what you think it means. It is "the LORD" who is a "man of war"—and the LORD (or Yahweh) is God's personal name, by which he revealed himself to Moses and his people (Exodus 3 v 13-17). It means "I AM WHO I AM" or "I WILL BE WHO I WILL BE." In the Bible what someone is called points to their character. And so God is saying, *I am all-sufficient and unchanging, and you will know who I am by what I do.*

So, if we're going to understand the Lord as a warrior in any kind of real, biblical way, we have to see how he "wars" throughout the biblical narrative.

In other words, because the LORD is a man of war, we can see the whole story of the world—past, present, and future—as the story of a cosmic war. The last chapter was about the God who you and I know; this one is about the story that you and I are living in—and, most importantly, the Warrior who is fighting and winning our battle.

And when we understand that story, we'll become excited about living in the days that we do, and we'll find a courage that can't be quenched and a confidence that can't be shaken—even by the end of Christendom.

HOW THINGS WERE AND HOW THINGS ARE

In the beginning, there was no war—only what the Hebrews called *shalom*. When God created everything that existed, he created it perfectly. It was "very good" (Genesis 1 v 31). Adam and Eve were naked and unashamed (Genesis 2 v 24). They had nothing to hide and felt no need to project a false image of themselves. They were what they were, and they were all good with what they were.

There was innocence, beauty, joy, wholeness—*shalom*.

On top of that, the whole created order was wired together perfectly: every star, every tree, every animal—there was perfect *shalom*. What we see now in this world, including even its most beautiful sights and sounds, is just a shadow or a shell of what it once was and what it eventually will be again.

We know this because the Bible tells us that right now...

"the creation waits with eager longing ... [to be] set free from its bondage to corruption and obtain the freedom of the glory of the children of God ... the whole creation has been groaning together..." (Romans 8 v 19, 21-22)

So this was the world of Genesis 1 – 2. Think of a symphony with all the instruments playing their parts. It was beautiful, rhythmic. It stirred the senses and the affections. It was *shalom*, and this is how God the Father created the world, through his Son and by his Spirit, to function.

But you're probably thinking, *Well, that's sweet, but this is not my week. This is not my world. My spouse and I fought. The dog chewed up my favorite book. My kid apparently can block out my voice. I've struggled with some anxiety. And that's before we get started with some of the craziness and news I saw on social media.*

That's the world we live in. It's marred. It's broken. How did we get from Genesis 1 and 2 to where we are now?

Well, it all starts with a story that supporters of Enlightenment thinking would not like because it can't be scientifically verified. Christianity is a religion that begins with God's revelation rather than with our reason. We do not believe in what is unreasonable, but we do accept things that cannot be reasoned out. And that's okay, because this is a revelation that was proved by a resurrection. That's why we believe in it and can stake our lives on it.

Scripture teaches us that there was a war in heaven. A particular angel, jealous of the glory of God, led a group of angels into battle against God in heaven. They lost (big surprise, right?), and they were cast out (Isaiah 14 v 12-15—this describes the fall of an ancient king, but uses language that seems too strong to refer to any merely human ruler; 2 Peter 2 v 4; Jude 6; Revelation 12 v 7-9). The angelic leader of that rebellion would come to be known as Satan—the devil.

Now back to our perfect garden—to *shalom*. Adam and Eve were walking in the cool of the garden, naked and unashamed. Then the serpent, Satan, said to Eve, "Did God actually say, 'You shall not eat of any tree in the garden?'" (Genesis 3 v 1). Subtext: *Have you not realized what God is up to? God doesn't want you to be fulfilled. God doesn't want you to become like him. He is restricting you and holding you back.*

Eve takes the bait and eats the fruit from the only tree God had told them not to eat from. And Adam is—well, he's there, but *he's not doing anything*. He doesn't protect her or support her. It's like he's just standing there birdwatching or something: *Ooh, look, a blue jay. I named that, you know. What? Fruit? Thanks, I'd love some.*

So they both eat of the fruit that God has forbidden. They grasp at being God.

And, in that moment, sin enters the world and *shalom* fractures, and the symphony and beauty and rhythm of God's created order is shattered as everything dances to a different tune—one of decay and death.

In fact, the Bible shows us that relational harmony fractures instantaneously: the second they eat the fruit, the Bible says they realize they are naked and they cover up.

The next time they hear the Lord walking in the garden, Adam and Eve are fearful, and take part in the most futile game of hide-and-go-seek in the history of mankind:

"The man and his wife hid themselves from the presence of the Lord God among the trees." (Genesis 3 v 8)

You're just not going to hide from an all-knowing God. It's about as preposterous as little kids who lie on the floor and think, *I can't see them because my eyes are closed, so they can't see me.*

And you say, *You're in the middle of the floor, bud. I'm standing over you right now.*

As funny as that example might sound, this scene in Scripture couldn't be more heartbreaking. For the first time ever, shame takes hold of the human heart. They run and hide—and we've been running and hiding from our Creator ever since.

But God finds them, and he declares war. Yet he doesn't declare war on Adam and Eve, but rather, on the serpent. Even more surprisingly, he declares that the war will be won not over humanity but through humanity:

"The LORD God said to the serpent,
 'Because you have done this, cursed are you …
 I will put enmity between you and the woman,
 and between your offspring and her offspring;
 he shall bruise your head,
 and you shall bruise his heel.'" (Genesis 3 v 14, 15)

With *shalom* shattered, Adam and Eve experience the implications of that cosmic collapse, but they also experience the compassion of a loving God. He continues to care for them despite the fact that they, although made his image and stewards of his creation, join the rebellion. They feel naked and ashamed, so God makes them clothes (v 21).

This was God's big play. He would war against the enemy and he would rescue those who joined the enemy. He would eradicate sin and free sinners. We see that culminate in the person and work of Jesus Christ. That is what it means for God to be a warrior. He will defeat his enemy so that the world is not destroyed but restored.

And knowing our part (that we're sinners) and his part (that he's fighting for us) makes us both humble and bold. It means we never think too highly of ourselves, and we never think too little of what he might do for and with us.

GOD FIGHTS FOR HIS PEOPLE

In their book *God is a Warrior*, theologians Tremper Longman III and Daniel G. Reid detail this warrior attribute of the Lord all the way from creation to restoration. They break it down into what they call the (slightly surreal-sounding) "Five Cosmic Stages of God's Warrior Nature."

Since these two theologians are far smarter than me, I don't see the need to try and reinvent the wheel here.

The stages they've established give us a glimpse of our Warrior God, instilling in us the sort of courage we need right now.

In Stage One, *God fights for Israel.* The people of God are living as slaves in Egypt. They're enslaved. They're oppressed. And God fights to free his people. Every plague poured out on Egypt corresponds to an Egyptian god—false gods behind whom lies the father of lies: the enemy, the devil. God actively kills false gods that enslave people.

The Egyptians worshiped the Nile, so God turned its waters to blood. They worshiped cattle, so he killed the livestock. They worshiped the god of the crops, so God sent locusts to devour the crops. They worshiped the sun god Ra, so God blacked out the sky and made it pitch black.

God literally wiped out the Egyptian gods, exposing them for what they were (not gods at all), along with the Pharaoh who worshiped them. And he led his people through the Red Sea and the wilderness, and into Canaan, the land he promised.

He promises their leader, Joshua, Moses' successor:

> *"No man shall be able to stand before you ... Be strong and courageous, for you shall cause this people to inherit the land that I swore to their fathers to give them ... Be strong and courageous. Do not be frightened, and do not be dismayed, for the LORD your God is with you wherever you go."*
>
> *(Joshua 1 v 5, 6, 9)*

God gives his people victory, and indeed no man can stand before the Israelite army, and they take the land God has promised to give them and to bless them in. They move back toward *shalom*.

Now this conquest of Canaan seems to be the ace of spades, the trump card, played by anyone wanting to discredit Christianity. Richard Dawkins plays this card in *The God Delusion*:

"The Bible is a blueprint of in-group morality, complete with instructions for genocide, enslavement of out-groups, and world domination."

Though Richard Dawkins is a brilliant intellect, I wonder if he's ever studied the Bible. Imagine going to a beach and watching a twenty-something-year-old running down the shore, killing everyone. You would say, *What a monster. This kid is a murderer and a maniac.*

But now imagine I tell you that this beach is in Normandy and the date is June 6, 1944—D-Day. The Allies are landing to reconquer Europe from the German armies. Now that young man is no longer a monster. He's a soldier and a liberator.

That's what was going on in Joshua's time. The Bible tells us that God gave the Canaanites 400 years to repent: to turn away from the type of idolatrous worship where babies were sacrificed to made-up gods, and where the elderly were killed because they lacked any good purpose in society, where anyone with any deformity was put to death. For four hundred years (that's essentially twice the length of time the United States has existed) God called the people of those lands to repent. They refused.

So God warred against the Canaanites, and he continued to fight for his people. He defeated his enemies, delivered his people, and dwelled with them.

GOD FIGHTS AGAINST HIS PEOPLE

In Stage Two, things take a turn—*God fights against Israel in judgment*. He had previously fought for Israel—now he fights against Israel! Why? Because as soon Israel gets out of Egypt and into the promised land, they begin to worship the pagan gods that they have been sent to destroy. They begin to do the same things that these people who had been judged by God had done.

As Adam and Eve did in the garden, so the Israelites did in the land, betraying and rebelling against God.

So God sent prophets and pleaded with the people to return to the good and beautiful design of his "Thou shalts" and "Thou shalt nots" so that joy, flourishing, and justice would return. They refused, and God warred against them.

Throughout the Old Testament, there were times when the people of God cried out to him, and he rescued and restored them; but the general theme was that of rebellion, of forgetting, of wandering.

This eventually led to the exile from the land. Prophets like Jeremiah warned, *Listen, if we do not repent, God is going to scatter us across the world. We will no longer have a place of our own. We will be scattered.* Sure enough, the people of God were scattered throughout the ancient world.

And so by Jesus' day, the descendants of Israel were dispersed across the Roman Empire, with little communities of faith in almost every major city and town in the known world.

THE HOPE OF A WARRIOR TO COME

In Stage Three, amid a period of waiting and silence, *the Israelites long for a savior*—the divine Warrior. Living in exile and captivity, they await a Messiah who will show up and restore his kingdom and his people. And they begin to get a vision of what is to come, giving them a hope and confidence despite their difficult circumstances.

The book of Daniel, chapter 7, paints a picture of God at war—an epic battle with four monsters of the sea. And in Zechariah, another piece of apocalyptic literature, the people of God are given yet another image of future hope—a great battle where the divine Warrior leads a vast army and overcomes his enemies.

The Israelites are able to look forward, remembering that the God who once fought for them will do so once again.

JESUS' CAMPAIGN OF DISARMAMENT

In Stage Four, as we get to the New Testament, *the Warrior God emerges*—and his name is Jesus.

The Son of God takes on flesh to defeat the power of sin, death, and Satan, and to rescue his people from the deadly consequences of their rebellion against the Creator. Yet this warfare doesn't fit the framework of what Israel expected.

It doesn't look like violence and destruction.

It doesn't come through power and conquest.

It comes through humility and weakness—through the cross.

When we think of Jesus' death, we tend to think of something like Colossians 2 v 13-14:

"You, who were dead in your trespasses and the uncircumcision of your flesh, God made alive together with him, having forgiven us all our trespasses, by canceling the record of debt that stood against us with its legal demands. This he set aside, nailing it to the cross."

In other words, when we think of salvation we usually think of personal salvation. It's what King David—and later Bono—sang about in the Psalm 40:

"The LORD ... heard my cry. He lifted me up from the pit of destruction, out of the miry bog, and set my feet upon a rock ...

He put a new song in my mouth, a song of praise to our God."
(v 1-3)

But there was more happening at the cross than mere personal salvation. It's about more—though never less—than you or me getting forgiveness from our sins and a restored relationship with God.

We often forget that Colossians 2 goes on to say:

"He disarmed the rulers and authorities and put them to open shame, by triumphing over them in him." (v 15)

Paul is talking about cosmic realities. The "rulers and authorities" are Satan and his demons. And they are "put ... to open shame" because they are shown to be toothless, disarmed.

After all, what is Satan's weapon, against which every human has no defense? It is our sin, for our sin allows Satan to accuse us before God of cosmic treason against God: of seeking to clamber onto his throne. If it were not for Christ's death, we would have no answer to that accusation.

But Christ died for our sins—he was punished for our cosmic treason—so that we might come back under his rule, be forgiven and glorify our King forever. At the cross, Satan's greatest weapon was put beyond use. When he accuses us of sin, the cross is our answer and our defense—and Satan has nothing left to say. The cross reveals him as publicly defeated.

Christ came and Christ defeated the devil. He crushed the head of the serpent even while the serpent bruised his heel (Genesis 3 v 15). And Christ tramples on his adversary every time a sinner comes to the cross, repents and believes, and passes from the dominion of darkness into the kingdom of light.

Satan has no accusation to bring against those who, through the work of the Spirit, are in Christ. The enemy has no foothold, no chance—not because they are not sinners but because they are now saved.

There is no sin, no scheme of Satan, with more power than the cross of Christ. There is no one who has gone too far. You can't out-sin the grace of God.

JOINING IN WITH HIS VICTORY

And so now, person by person, *the church takes the victory out to the world* as we proclaim the gospel of Christ. Speaking of the mission of the church, Paul says:

"Through the church the manifold wisdom of God might now be made known to the rulers and authorities in the heavenly places." (Ephesians 3 v 10)

What God is doing in the church—what God is doing in *your* church—is revealing his wisdom not just to mankind (to whom the church may look very foolish) but to spiritual powers and authorities and rulers.

You know what that means? Every time a local church, made up of saved sinners, gathers to celebrate the gospel and goes out to proclaim the gospel, God's unsearchable wisdom and God's unstoppable victory is put on display to the spiritual forces. Satan is reminded of his defeat every time your church meets. There's something incredible about that—the church revealing the bankruptcy and futility of Satan's plans in the heavenly realms.

But all too often, we forget about these cosmic realities and the power of the church.

C.S. Lewis's *The Screwtape Letters* is a brilliant book about an older demon, Screwtape, discipling a younger demon named Wormwood on how to deceive a man who is his "patient." Wormwood has allowed his client to become a Christian, so the older demon is counseling Wormwood about how to pull this man away from his faith. And Lewis puts these words in Screwtape's mouth:

"One of our great allies at present is the Church itself. Do not misunderstand me. I do not mean the Church as we see her spread out through all time and space and rooted in eternity, terrible as an army with banners ... fortunately [that] is quite invisible to these humans ... Provided that any of those neighbors [sitting near him in church] sing out of tune, or have boots that squeak, or double chins, or odd clothes, the patient will quite easily believe that their religion must therefore be somehow ridiculous."

Don't we fall for this trick? How easy it is to forget this grand vision and reality of our churches and focus instead on the frustrations or the flaws, becoming blind to those cosmic realities. Here is what we must remember and enjoy. Today the church is joining in the victory of our Warrior God by living out the gospel wherever we are, using the weapons of compassion, of mercy, of faithful, loving presence in the fight. We have been invited by God to reign and rule with him through Christ, pushing back darkness and beckoning people into the light.

JESUS WINS

In Stage Five, *Jesus will return again as a warrior* to fight the final battle against his enemies:

"Then I saw heaven opened, and behold, a white horse! The one sitting on it is called Faithful and True, and in righteousness he judges and makes war. His eyes are like a flame of fire, and on his head are many diadems, and he has a name written that no one knows but himself. He is clothed in a robe dipped in blood, and the name by which he is called is The Word of God. And the armies of heaven, arrayed in fine linen, white and pure, were following him on white horses. From his mouth comes a sharp sword with which to strike down the nations, and he will rule them with a rod of iron. He will tread the winepress of the fury of the wrath of God the Almighty. On his robe and on his thigh he has a name written, King of kings and Lord of lords." (Revelation 19 v 11-16)

This is a far cry from 6-pound, 3-ounce baby Jesus. This is a Jesus who fights. And it is not a long battle. Jesus returns, defeats those who have refused to come under his rule, and enjoys the *shalom* of his reign.

Then we return to what we read in Genesis 1 and 2—except now it's even better: a beautiful, perfect, eternal garden-city that Revelation 21 – 22 pictures. The prophet Isaiah portrays the deserts blooming with flowers, the mountaintops producing sweet wine, and the lamb and the wolf laying down together (Isaiah 35 v 1-2; 25 v 6-8; 65 v 25). It's creation remade. Every man and woman on earth will bring glory to this triune God. You will bring glory to this God by being an object of his grace, putting the enemy to open shame—or you'll be an object of his just, right wrath.

That's what makes this God so terrifying.

Is he loving? Yes.

Gracious? Yes.

Merciful? Yes.

Long-suffering? Absolutely.

Tinker Bell? Not at all. Not at all.

He is a Warrior, and he fights for his people, and he wins.

THIS IS THE STORY

This world is full of stories. All those Netflix binges you go on... all the sports that you keep up with on your television, your phone, your computer, and your radio... all these sorts of things that we consume and enjoy for our entertainment are telling us a story about ourselves, about our world, about our future, and, yes, about God.

They're discipling us, every day, shaping and forming us.

Whether we realize it or not, we are being shaped and formed by the movies and TV shows we watch, the music, podcasts and radio stations we listen to, the books and magazines that we read, the social media feeds that we skim, and the trips we take to the mall. To the extent that we choose to listen uncritically to them and live in them, the stories of our culture are changing us.

If we're not careful, we'll look at what lies before us— this age of unbelief—and let these other stories shape not only the way that we see it but also the way that we respond to it. We'll live in those stories, and we'll shrink back or sell out. But praise God: we have a true and better story to live in—the story of God the Warrior, the greatest story ever told!

Everything about your life fits inside this story. This is *the* story. It doesn't matter what you do. If you're a welder or a businesswoman or a doctor or a teacher or a garbage man, this is *your* story. This is the only cause worth living for and fighting for and denying our comforts for and, yes, dying for.

Listen: the church is on the right side of history because we are on the side of the Lord of history. We are often accused of being old-fashioned and beyond our expiration date. That will only increase in our post-Christendom age. But in truth our time has yet to come, and the gospel has never been in fashion in a world rebelling against its Maker. The arc of history bends toward the justice and peace and triumph of Christ's return, and that is the story and the message and the confidence of the church. We know the result of the battle that has raged since creation and the fall, and that was won on the cross, and that will end with the divine Warrior's return.

Since we know the end, we live toward it.

We draw courage from it.

We take heart in it.

We do not wring our hands over the progress of some culture war if we know the result of *the* cosmic war.

And we do not navel-gaze or keep our heads down if we know our role in that war—to take out the gospel declaration of victory won and victory offered, pushing back the darkness where we are, in what we do and what we say, day by day by day, until *the* day.

5. HOW IT LOOKS

What does courage actually look like? Once we become emboldened with a God-sized courage, how does that bear on our everyday lives?

Well, I'm glad you asked. That's what the rest of this book is about, and there is no better place to start our answer than with a letter written to believers on the margins of society, experiencing pain and persecution for their faith. 1 Peter gives us a compelling picture of Christian courage in an age of unbelief.

DEAR EXILES

The context of the group of churches that Peter is writing to isn't that much different than that of Romans. Of course, Paul isn't the writer. It's the apostle Peter—the same guy who denied Christ three times yet became a pillar of the church (that's for free, in case you're ever doubting the sufficiency of God's grace on your life). But this group of Christians are in a similar boat to those Paul wrote in Rome. Spread across Asia Minor, living under the rule of the Roman Empire three hundred years before things turned around and Christianity became the official religion of the empire, these believers were living in a world that was socially hostile at best and physically violent at worst.

History tells us things got a lot worse for these churches before they got easier. See 1 Peter as the Spirit preparing God's people for what he knew was coming next.

Lord willing, we won't face the immense amount of suffering that the early church did, but I know we're headed further and further toward the margins. I know that, at the very least, the idea that Christians are bigots and idiots isn't going away—things are only getting worse. I know I'm from Texas, and everyone here was essentially born inside a church, but even here, we can already feel a subtle shift in the way that Christians are perceived and treated. And that's in Texas, where there's basically a church on every block. If you're reading this in Seattle or New York, or most anywhere in Europe, you get this more than I do.

Peter told his first readers that they were "sojourners and exiles" (2 v 11): outcasts and misfits who did not belong— and that wouldn't have been news to them. They only had to consider the way they were being treated to see that. That's why 1 Peter resonates with us so much today. It's a part of Scripture that may have sounded strange at the height of Christendom, but certainly doesn't now. We too are exiles because this world is not our home; we too are beginning to find that others "speak against [us] as evildoers" (2 v 12); and we too find ourselves stepping into a season of winter.

WHERE TO STAND AND WHERE TO LOOK

Peter knows where he is in the great story of what our Warrior God is doing.

Peter knows that Satan is defeated but not yet crushed, and that the church is to exist as a light that pushes back the darkness, despite Satan's best efforts to thwart Jesus' victory, in person after person as they come to faith and continue in the faith.

Read what he says in 5 v 8-12, remembering that we live after Christ's death and resurrection, and before he finally defeats his enemy:

"Be sober-minded; be watchful. Your adversary the devil prowls around like a roaring lion, seeking someone to devour. Resist him, firm in your faith, knowing that the same kinds of suffering are being experienced by your brotherhood throughout the world. And after you have suffered a little while, the God of all grace, who has called you to his eternal glory in Christ, will himself restore, confirm, strengthen, and establish you. To him be the dominion forever and ever. Amen."

Satan is still fighting. And he wants to "devour" us. If he can make us give way to fear—if he can convince us that the age of unbelief means the Christian church is done—then he can devour our faith and he can drag us down with him.

So Peter says: *Resist him.*

And we say: *How?*

We must do two things: we must stand firm on grace and we must look forward to eternity.

"Resist him, firm in your faith" (v 9), says Peter; that is, our faith in "the God of all grace" (v 10). Peter puts it all together as he sums up his whole reason for writing:

"I have written briefly to you, exhorting and declaring that this is the true grace of God. Stand firm in it." (v 12)

We resist the temptation to give in to fear and faithlessness by planting our feet on the ground of the grace of God. Here's how this works.

Grace tells you that you are loved by the Creator of everything, forgiven by the Judge of everything, overseen by the Sovereign of everything, and privileged to be used by the Sustainer of everything.

Grace says that we are "a chosen people," God's special possession (2 v 9, NIV).

Grace says that there is nothing you can do to earn more of God's love, and there is nothing you can do to lose God's love.

When Satan says you're worthless, grace says you're valuable.

When Satan says you're useless, grace says yes, but you're forgiven now.

When Satan says he's taking everything worth having away from you, grace says he can never take what you most need—God.

When Satan says you can't win, grace reminds you that Jesus already won.

Grace laughs in Satan's face, grace overcomes fear, grace breeds courage.

So this is where we live. We just stand on grace. And when we fail, we get right back up and stand on grace again—because, from there, we are able to look forward to eternity with the rock-solid confidence that we are God's forgiven people, walking home to "an inheritance that is imperishable, undefiled, and unfading, kept in heaven for you" (1 v 4).

We will be marginalized. We will be mocked. We may even be persecuted and killed. Peter's letter was written to a church facing all that. And did you notice how he talks about such trials? "After you have suffered a little while..." (5 v 10).

A little while? Why does he call it that? Because, compared to eternity, this lifetime is a blink. It's just a blink. Satan wants us to focus on the blink—and our blink is looking hard in this age of unbelief. Grace points us forwards to look to eternity. Grace reminds us that whatever we face now, we can walk through it with living hope and joy and courage, for "the God of all grace [has] called you to his eternal glory in Christ" (v 10).

And we know that this future is certain because God "has caused us to be born again to a living hope through the resurrection of Jesus Christ from the dead" (1 v 3). The resurrection is fundamental because it proves that the final cosmic stage will come—that eternity really does lie ahead.

Without the resurrection, our faith is in vain and our courage will fail.

With the resurrection, we can stand firm.

We may live in an age of unbelief but we are headed for an eternity of unimaginable glory with our Savior. Jesus has risen. *Stand on grace,* Peter says, *and look to eternity.*

HOW SHOULD WE THEN LIVE?

Okay, but this still raises the question: once you have hope, once you have courage, what does life look like? You've begun to grasp the greatness of God… you've begun to get excited by the story and your part in it… you're looking forward to eternity as you stand on grace… now, as the Christian thinker Francis Schaeffer said, "How should we then live?"

To be sure, the main aim of this book is not to create some sort of one-size-fits-all blueprint for living faithfully in this age of unbelief. What I'm calling for here is a not a strategy but a posture—a state of the head and heart—motivated by courage. Yet I'd be cruel to completely leave you hanging, right? Thankfully, 1 Peter breaks this down for us:

"As obedient children, do not be conformed to the passions of your former ignorance, but as he who called you is holy, you also be holy in all your conduct, since it is written, 'You shall be holy, for I am holy.' And if you call on him as Father who judges impartially according to each one's deeds, conduct yourselves with fear throughout the time of your exile."

(1 v 14-17)

The first implication or result of courage is holiness.

When we have hope and confidence that the Lord knows best, and that his story is the one, true story that gives us life and purpose and joy, we're not as likely to give in to the temptation to be squeezed into what our culture says is acceptable or praiseworthy. We won't be, as Paul put it, "conformed to this world" (Romans 12 v 2). Instead, we care more for what our Father thinks than what our culture thinks. We obey his word, not our society's ways. God-sized courage pursues God-like holiness.

And holiness looks like integrity.

Let me give you just one example. There's a woman in my church who was climbing the ladder in her industry and doing very well. She's a smart, educated woman and she was headed for the top (and, trust me, she was going to get there). Then she ran into a supervisor who was doing some things that were shady at best and illegal at worst. She knew that to do those things, going against her conscience, would then make her a part of what was displeasing to the Lord. But, at the same time, what she was making in her job was key for her family. I don't mean it was key for them being able to have a long vacation in the summer. I mean it was key for her family's ability to pay their bills and have food to eat.

Yet, despite the dilemma confronting her, she reported the illegal activity. She resigned from her position. She testified to her co-workers, and then she walked away. In the economy at that point, it was hard to find another job. It took a while. In that time, life shrunk down. It was hard.

She was walking without wealth, and she was walking without a career, but she was walking with integrity.

That's courage. It's ordinary Christians living in a way that is empowered by something that transcends our current situation, especially the fears felt in this age of unbelief. If we walk in awe of God, our Father and our Judge, the God of deep riches and wisdom and knowledge, then we'll walk with courage and integrity.

Courage means we look different and distinct. It means we live righteous lives. It means we don't deal with people in shady ways. We let people know we're living and working for something that's bigger than us and that's bigger than that paycheck. There is something—Someone—far greater and more important than our career, our reputation, or even our safety.

Courage pursues holiness and that looks like integrity.

THE COURAGE TO SEEK GOOD

Next, courage looks like devotion—first to our church, and second to the common good.

Don't believe that old lie of Christendom that, when it comes to mission and ministry, there are professionals and non-professionals; and if I pay my fees, then I can leave the heavy lifting to the ones who get the checks for doing it. Not many of us would actually admit or verbalize that, but we often operate from this mentality. As a pastor I see this so often. Peter tells us that:

"Having purified your souls by your obedience to the truth for a sincere brotherly love, love one another earnestly from a pure heart." (1 v 22)

When we have Christian courage, we are prepared to take the risk of loving one another. We take the gospel to those who need to hear it, rather than bringing people to hear the professionals do their thing. We speak the gospel to our brothers and sisters who need to be encouraged by it or pressed with it, rather than leaving it to the professionals to do their thing.

Devotion requires me to bear the cost of putting my time, my energy, my money, my service, my mind, and my heart at the service of my brothers and sisters in the family of God.

But courage not only drives us to love one another, as the body of Christ. That devotion also overflows into the way we interact with our neighbors, communities, cities, and this world—and it bleeds into the way we engage with culture and politics. So Peter says:

"Be subject for the Lord's sake to every human institution, whether it be to the emperor as supreme, or to governors as sent by him to punish those who do evil and to praise those who do good … Honor everyone. Love the brotherhood. Fear God. Honor the emperor." (2 v 13-17)

You may think it's hard to "honor the emperor" right now. Many believers aren't even trying. But don't forget that it was harder for those who first read these words to honor their ruler in their conduct and speech. Their emperor was setting his face against their faith and using his power to persecute them. But they had not set their hopes on the emperor, nor on their own reputations or safety. Their hope was in a risen King and a certain eternity.

They knew what story they lived in.

And when we find our courage in this God and in that story, we are freed up to love openly and graciously.

As Christians, we don't need to "win" when it comes to

politics. We don't need to tie our hopes to one party or react with fury when the other guy gets in, as though some mere human might thwart God's plans—as though God sits in heaven and says, *Oh, this democratic system is really messing things up. I can't achieve my plans now they voted for that one. They were meant to choose the other way!* As the pastor Juan Sanchez puts it in his book *1 Peter For You*:

"Our sovereign Lord knows what he is doing. Just as he wastes no suffering, he also doesn't waste any government appointment. We may not understand why a particular person is in power, but we can rest assured that our King does."

After all, this is his story, the end is already certain, and he is writing the script.

When we operate out of fear, we view the political arena as a place in which to legislate and control morality, or as a way to gain control of our world to protect ourselves, or as something altogether evil to be shunned. But those who operate out of courage see politics as a way to seek the common good, to promote human flourishing, and ultimately to love others.

Courage gives us the ability, in this age of unbelief, to speak positively and seek unity, to love those who disagree with us and seek to malign us, to be unsurprised and not angered when a society that rejects Christ does not line up its laws with those of Christ—and to keep on loving and seeking to bless.

That takes far more courage than opting out or getting mad.

THE COURAGE TO SPEAK TRUTH

Whereas the grace and hope given to us in Christ serves as the foundation for 1 Peter and for our courage as Christians, the letter itself moves toward stewardship of that grace and hope, ultimately culminating in a call to share that grace and hope.

In other words, courage looks like evangelism.

I mean, is there a better way to love our brothers and sisters than to push and point them toward Christ? Is there a better way to love our neighbors—and, yes, our enemies—than to seek to lead them to Christ? Is there anything more unloving than to do everything else we've mentioned yet to miss this piece?

We'll dig deeper into this idea in the next chapter, but I think it's essential to address here because, well, Peter does! In fact, he connects our witness to having a right view of Jesus Christ:

"In your hearts honor Christ the Lord as holy, always being prepared to make a defense to anyone who asks you for a reason for the hope that is in you." (3 v 15)

We live in a time when, as the British pastor and evangelist Rico Tice describes,

"There is increasing hostility to the gospel message. But there is something else going on, too. There is also increased hunger. The same rising tide of secularism and materialism that rejects truth claims and is offended by absolute moral standards is proving to be an empty and hollow way to live ... you're more and more likely to find people quietly hungering for the content of the gospel, even as our culture teaches them to be hostile towards it."
(Honest Evangelism)

I know that, on the surface, it seems that everyone these days despises Christians, and thinks we're a bunch of uneducated philistines who are stuck in the past. Generally speaking, we are living in an age of unbelief. But that doesn't mean that everyone is a staunch atheist dead set on the belief that there is absolutely no God and nothing beyond the surface. In some ways, I think folks are as curious as ever.

There's a longing for more than the material, a yearning for something beyond. Whether it's TV shows like *Stranger Things* and *The Leftovers* or movies like *Arrival* and the billion superhero films that have come out in the last decade, what we choose to watch suggests that we're a people plagued with skepticism and cynicism, yet haunted by the transcendent, by the extraordinary.

I say all that to make this point: I think people are willing to have spiritual conversations. People are looking for opportunities to talk about spirituality and eternity. Despite their doubts and reservations, people are ready to ask you "for a reason for the hope that is in you," sometimes with a note of aggression, and at other times with a sense of wistfulness that you have what they would like and cannot find.

And, when that happens, Peter commands us to be "prepared to make a defense to anyone who asks." We have to risk the hostility to find the hunger. That will, of course, take courage, but we know that we have courage in a God who is different than us, not constrained like us, and glorious in his riches and his wisdom and his knowledge.

We tend to make this more complicated than it needs to be. Here's how courage might look. You will say to someone you know well:

"Hey, man, will you forgive me?"

"For what?"

"I've known you for years, and maybe it has been my own lack of courage or maybe I didn't want to risk this friendship, but honestly, I'd love to tell you about my relationship with Jesus and what God has done in my life."

It doesn't have to be complicated. It doesn't have to be difficult. We don't have to have all the right things to say or the perfect delivery or anything. But it will take courage.

And, thankfully, we can find that courage in the Lord.

Christian courage in the twenty-first century looks like it did in the first. It looks the same in our post-Christendom

West as it did in the pre-Christendom Roman Empire. It looks like holiness and integrity, it looks like devotion to one another and to others in every sphere of life, and it looks like evangelism. And that brings us to our next chapter, and to one very surprising place where we display our Christian courage in the age of unbelief.

6. THE SURPRISING PLACE YOU'LL SHOW YOUR COURAGE

I can't say it too many times: the point of this book is not to present some fresh strategy for how we might live in these challenging times—this isn't the "Chandler Option."

No, the aim is to give you a big enough view of God—of God the Warrior, who is infinite in his knowledge and wisdom and riches, and who has already written the end of the story—for you to be empowered to live with faithful, joyful, positive courage in our secular, post-Christian, post-whatever world.

But, as we began to see from 1 Peter in the last chapter, that kind of courage does work out in practical and radical ways, day in and day out in our ordinary lives. Now I want to take that even further. I want to continue painting a picture of courage and pull this whole idea down to the ground and talk more about what it looks like in your life practically. I think you'll be surprised at what it means for your every day.

ALL AUTHORITY

Though you may be surprised by where we end up, we are starting in a familiar place—the Great Commission in Matthew 28 v 18-20:

"And Jesus came and said to them, 'All authority in heaven and on earth has been given to me. Go therefore and make disciples of all nations, baptizing them in the name of the Father and of the Son and of the Holy Spirit, teaching them to observe all that I have commanded you. And behold, I am with you always, to the end of the age.'"

I want to dig into the latter half, but before going any further, it can't be overstated just how important the first part is.

Even as he gives his people their marching orders, Jesus reminds them of where Christian courage comes from. Before giving his disciples any command, Jesus recognizes just how challenging it will be to obey what he's about to call them to, and so he reminds them that he is bigger than anything we will face.

Every time I'm reminded that "all authority in heaven and on earth" has been given to Jesus, I like to stop right there and think, *Okay, Chandler, whatever he says next—you're going to be all right*. If all authority in heaven and on earth have been given to Jesus, and he's my Lord, well, however things work out, they'll work out all right for me because I'm his, and he has all authority—everywhere, for all time.

I need to know that, and you need to know that, and that's the basis for every practical way we seek to obey this command.

WE HAVE TO GO

But we do need to get practical—because Jesus tells us to "go."

I know it's hard to believe that Christians would make a big fuss and disagree on something, but there's actually an argument over what is going on with that word "go," and I think that actually both sides are arguing for the same thing, but kind of missing each other (Christians like to make everything "either/or," when truly most things are "both/and," but now I'm getting off topic). If you're married, you know what I'm talking about—you'll know there are times when you and your spouse are both saying the same thing, but somehow you're not realizing that you are.

So one side of this argument says, *Okay, what this command means is that you go. You get all your stuff and head out. You go into all the nations. You pack up your stuff, you leave your land, and you go into a land where Christ is not known and preach and teach the gospel there.*

I think that's exactly what Jesus is saying here.

But the other side of the argument comes back and says that actually, the word "go" in the Greek carries a meaning that is more like, "As you go, therefore..." So it's not that you actually pack up and move, like a missionary would, but rather, that all of us should be on mission in our homes, at our jobs, in our communities, and so on.

I think that's also exactly what Jesus is saying here.

I don't believe all Christians are missionaries—not in the sense that some Christians are called to be those who leave their land and head to a different culture in a different place in the world to herald the good news of the gospel. That's not for all of us. But I do I believe that all Christians live on mission. Some pack up their stuff and leave. Others stay right where they are. But both dedicate their lives to the mission of God, pushing back what's dark to seek and save the lost.

So whether you pack up and go overseas or whether you are going about your normal life three blocks from where you grew up, the command is the same:

"Make disciples of all nations, baptizing them in the name of the Father and of the Son and of the Holy Spirit, teaching them to observe all that I have commanded you."

Remember how God is going to accomplish his plan in Stage Four of the cosmic battle—through his church, through his people. His plan will be fulfilled. He has all authority. But the way that plan will be fulfilled is through you and me courageously living and speaking his gospel. I don't know about you, but that's a pretty amazing thing to wrap your head around.

We are commanded to make followers of Jesus. But that is not an easy call. The reason why Jesus assures us that "I am with you always" is because it may sometimes feel like he isn't, and because it should always be obvious to us that we need him to be with us in whatever we are doing. By the Holy Spirit, he goes with us as we go—but in order for him to go with us, we do need to go, whether that involves going overseas or across the street.

COURAGE IS GOING TO LOOK LIKE...

By now you're probably thinking, *Okay Pastor Matt* (for what it's worth, hardly anyone actually calls me that), *that's well and good. Thanks for reminding me about the Great Commission. But what does all this have to do with the end of Christendom and the need for courage?*

Here's what: when we talk about our lives and our responses and what it means to be courageous and faithful in the age of unbelief, we have to talk about the Great Commission. That's our mission. That's the Christian life. Everything we do comes back to that. And remember, according to 1 Peter, one thing courage looks like, along with holy integrity and devotion, is evangelism.

Which means—in all times and places, but perhaps particularly in this age of unbelief—courage is going to look like hospitality.

You heard me right.

Courageous living looks like showing hospitality.

Don't hear me say that hospitality is the sum total of courage (or of evangelism and discipleship, for that matter). But don't miss me saying that living courageously will involve living hospitably. And probably more than ever in this age of unbelief.

If hospitality doesn't sound exciting or initially feels confusing, that's because the idea of hospitality got hijacked by Martha Stewart, and became less about a way we live our lives and more about how we decorate and prepare meals for the holiday seasons. I'm not against that. But I am saying that's not what the Bible means when it talks about hospitality.

When the Bible speaks of hospitality, it almost always ties it to aliens and strangers—that is, to people who are not like us. If I had to come up with a biblical definition for hospitality, I'd say it means *to give loving welcome to those outside your normal circle of friends*. It is opening your life and your house to those who believe differently than you do. And the Bible is serious about hospitality:

"Do not neglect to show hospitality to strangers, for thereby some have entertained angels unawares." (Hebrews 13 v 1-2)

(I don't know what that looks like, but it sounds awesome. By showing hospitality to strangers we may entertain angels without knowing it.)

Hospitality is so important to God that when Paul lists out the traits necessary for a man to be qualified for the office of elder in a local congregation, we find that he must be...

"... above reproach, the husband of one wife, sober-minded, self-controlled, respectable, hospitable, able to teach..."
(1 Timothy 3 v 2)

Most of that list makes sense. Above reproach... the husband of one wife... able to teach. Who's going to say, *That guy who everyone knows can't be trusted, he should lead us. The guy who's kind of half in on his wife, he should be an elder. The guy who can't teach the Bible at all and has no idea what it says, let's ask him to preach to us?* Those things are obvious.

But hospitable? To be an elder, a man has to be able to open his life and show kindness to those who believe differently than he does? He has to open up his world to those who are outside of what he believes and what he senses? Yes. This is serious. It really is.

Now why would the Bible talk so seriously about hospitality?

Well, if I could just boil it all down to its simplest truth, it's because God has been so hospitable to us. Even when we were living as his enemies, God came and saved us. Through the work of his Son, the Father opened the door and invited us into his presence through his indwelling Spirit. God has shown his kindness to us over and over and over again, despite us being outsiders and strangers, despite us being outside the promises, despite us being in rebellion against him.

God shows hospitality to his enemies in saving us as sinners and inviting us to eat at his table in his eternal home.

We demonstrate that we truly appreciate the divine hospitality we have received as we extend our own hospitality to those around us. My friend John Piper says (look up his 1985 sermon *Strategic Hospitality* at desiringgod.org):

"When we practice hospitality, here's what happens: we experience the refreshing joy of becoming conduits of God's hospitality rather than being self-decaying cul-de-sacs. The joy of receiving God's hospitality decays and dies if it doesn't flourish in our own hospitality to others."

I'm not suggesting that biblical hospitality is the silver bullet for making evangelism work in the 21st century (news flash: there is no silver bullet). I'm not saying that if the church behaves this way, the world will do a 180 and magically start to think highly of us again. It won't. But having said that, might it not be, in our cynical, polarizing, critical culture, that a warm dose of welcoming hospitality will take some folks by surprise and open up the door for opportunities to make disciples of Jesus Christ?

FOUR WAYS TO SHOW HOSPITALITY

The triune God of the cosmos is serious about hospitality. Hospitality can create an entry point for living out the Great Commission and evangelizing our neighbors, especially in the age of unbelief, when most think the church is about something completely different. Yet we still have to ask: how do we show hospitality today?

It's not complicated—though that doesn't mean it's easy.

Number one: welcome everyone you meet.

One of the things I teach my children is, when they meet people, to shake their hand and look at them in the eyes and tell them their name and ask the person for their name. That might sound like something you'd hear on *Leave it to Beaver* or *The Andy Griffith Show*, and probably makes you think of the supposedly good ol' days of Christendom. But that's not the point. The point is that in doing this we show others, especially those who don't look like us and talk like us, that we see them and value them as people— as men and women created in God's image.

So, literally, I think the best thing to do is greet everyone you see. That's an easy thing to do if you are wired like me—I'm a grade-A extrovert. That's hard if you're an introvert, and right now you're thinking, *Can we just go to number two, please?* But often the best things to do are the hardest things to do. Pray for grace, ask for strength and, well, greet people.

Number two: engage with people.

Remember that everyone you meet is eternal. You have never met someone who will cease to exist one day, and you have never met someone who does not bear God's image. So care about and take an interest in those you run across.

I don't think this is overly difficult. It simply needs us to be asking open-ended questions, letting our inner curiosity out:

"What do you do?"

"I'm a controller."

"Okay, what's a controller? What does the week of a controller look like? What do you do on Monday? Do you control stuff? How does this work? Okay, is Tuesday any different? Do you have a day that's very different?"

You may think this is all obvious—but often we hold back from doing it. You need to get to know people, take an interest in them, and listen to them, rather than just trying to think about how you can say something memorable or hilarious.

"Tell me about your life. How long have you been married? How did you guys meet? What do you find great about marriage? Any difficult times? Any painful points?"

You read that and you think, *Wow, that's really personal*. I think you'd be surprised (obviously taking account of your particular culture) at how willing people are to engage at that level because we live in a world where everyone knows everyone, but no one really knows anyone. We live in a world where I have hundreds of Facebook friends and no one who will speak truth into my life or to whom I can turn when I have messed up or need wise counsel. People are really hungry to be known and really hungry for conversation that goes deeper than how we think the Dallas Cowboys are going to do this year. Engage with people where they are.

Number three: make dinner a priority.

The Bible, over and over again, talks about the holiness of eating together. Long dinners with good food, good drink, good company, and good conversations that center around our beliefs, our hopes, our fears—that's a good dinner. The Bible says that's holy.

Think about how many significant moments in the Gospels happen around the dinner table.

A sinful woman finds forgiveness and a legalistic Pharisee gets his pride torn up (Luke 7 v 36-50).

Zacchaeus, the tax collector who had realized that his money had bought him only misery, discovered all the joy he needed in Jesus, and then sat with his Lord and announced that he would give away generously the wealth he had once grasped onto tightly (Luke 19 v 1-10).

Jesus' friend Mary poured out her devotion as she poured out her perfume on his feet while he sat and ate in her family home (John 12 v 1-3).

Our Lord gave us the visual "words" of the bread and wine of the Lord's Supper over his last dinner with his friends before he died (Luke 22 v 14-20).

A once-dead man, our risen Savior, ate fish with his friends and gave them their world-changing mission as he did so (Luke 24 v 36-49).

Dinners change lives. So make them a priority.

Oh, and I don't mean dinner with friends, by the way. Yes, eat with your church small group, and invite over your good friends, but remember that hospitality is *to give loving welcome to those outside your normal circle of friends*. It is opening your life and your home to those who believe differently than you do. Make dinner with these people whom God has placed near you a priority. Invite them into your life so that you might know them, engage them, love them, serve them and walk alongside them through a broken and shattered world, witnessing to them of the love of the One who died to invite them to his table.

Number four: in all of this, love the outsider.

In every work environment, every neighborhood, there are people who, for whatever reason, are kind of outliers. Maybe they just moved into the area, or into your state or country. Maybe they have struggles that they keep behind their front door or buried in their past, which mean they are just different and difficult. Maybe God just wired them differently, or life's disappointments have messed with that wiring. Whatever the case, these people definitely live near you and they definitely work with you. They're all around you—perhaps more so than ever, in our globalized world.

Now naturally, we think, *Yeah, I know that guy in our neighborhood. I know that mom whose kids are in the same class as mine. There's a reason they're outsiders. They're different. They're kind of weird. They're socially off. All the times I've tried to engage with them, they haven't seemed to be interested. I heard they are pretty messed up.*

I understand that you might feel that way, though you probably wouldn't say it out loud or anything. I get it. I've been there. Sometimes, I'm still there. Because of the way sin affects us, we tend to run away from differences and from being around people who think differently and look differently than us. Diversity isn't our default position. Sameness is. But I want to lay this before you:

Jesus Christ would have moved toward those people.

That's what you see in his ministry over and over. He eats with people no one else will eat with. He is hospitable to the outsiders.

After all, he moved toward you. You were an outsider. However awkward you find those around you who are outliers, that's nothing compared to the distance between the holy God and you:

"God shows his love for us in that while we were still sinners, Christ died for us." (Romans 5 v 8)

You were not good when Christ came for you. God the Son did not look at me and say, *Man, have you seen what great company Matt Chandler is? He's just like us, Father! We've got to have him to dinner here, for all eternity.* No, Matt Chandler was a sinner, an outsider, with nothing in common with the perfect Father, Son, and Spirit—and God saved me anyway. God extends radical hospitality to me and to you.

That's why we love the outsider: because we were the outsider. That's our story.

ENGAGING WITH A MUSLIM FAMILY

When I think about the hospitality that comes when we live with courage, I'm reminded of Afshin Ziafat, a good friend and a gifted pastor. Afshin's family moved to Houston, Texas, from Iran when he was just 6 years old. This was in the seventies, at the time of the Islamic Revolution and then the Iranian hostage crisis, which left a group of Americans hostage in Iran for a number of years.

Afshin's family didn't exactly get a warm welcome upon their arrival in the States. Folks threw rocks through the windows of their home. The tires of their cars were slashed. The family were harassed and threatened with physical violence—all because they were Muslims and from Iran.

But, at a time when the cultural climate was chaotic and Afshin's family felt alienated and abandoned given the general hostility toward Muslims and Iranians, there was at least one woman who was different—one woman who lived out courage.

Afshin's English tutor in elementary school acted differently than the other Americans his family came in contact with. Motivated by the gospel, this woman loved Afshin unconditionally. She poured herself into his life— not just teaching him the skills necessary to communicate in the English language, but also genuinely caring for him as a person made in the image of God.

She welcomed him, and his family. She engaged with them, giving her time and risking her reputation. She loved the outsider.

When he was in the 2nd grade, Afshin's tutor told him, *Afshin, I've been reading you all these books. Now I want to hand you the most important book you'll ever get in your life.* And she handed him a small copy of the New Testament.

Afshin didn't read this book for another ten years. He would never have read it at all if she hadn't given it to him. And he would likely never have read it at all if she had not also shown him hospitality first. But she did, and he did read it, and it was that New Testament that God used to bring him to faith.

This woman didn't give in to the anxieties prevalent in her cultural climate. She wasn't stunted and held back by the fear that this Muslim family was dangerous or that some new religion was taking over her country. Filled with the hope and courage of the Lord, she had an eternal perspective that moved her to love, compassion, and hospitality. Where others saw a threat, she saw an opportunity.

That's courage.

That's hospitality.

CONVERSATIONS ABOUT LIFE

Given my role as a pastor, I have to be really intentional about leaving my Christian bubble to enter into spaces where I'm surrounded by individuals who are not like me and who do not believe what I do.

One of the ways I've attempted to do this is through a thing called Book Club. Honestly, we probably need to rename it as something else, because often we don't read a book; we just go for an article or a blog post. But the purpose is to create an environment where, wherever we are on the spiritual spectrum, we can have conversations—not just about God, but about anything. It's a group of men who want to have conversations about life.

It's not always Christian books that we read. In fact, most of the books are far from that. I've read everything from a book about the crazy basketball coach Bobby Knight to a book about a hitman (I hid that one from my children because it so generously used the f-word).

I love this group of men, and my affection for them has grown so much over the years. That said, I would never bring my kids along. Book Club can be pretty grimy, honestly. Every meaningful conversation that we have is surrounded by inappropriate jokes that I wouldn't dare repeat in this book or at church.

And that's great—because I'm convinced that it's these sorts of spaces that we need to be playing in as Christians if we really are serious about the gospel. Yes and amen to keeping your guard up and being in a community of believers who can check you on things and hold you accountable. But biblical hospitality means welcoming those who are not like us—or rather, whose sinfulness displays itself in ways that are different than ours does.

We have to be willing to get outside our comfort zones, to get our hands dirty. Jesus did.

Sure, some of the conversations will be uncomfortable. Sure, sometimes things will get a little tense. That's certainly been true of Book Club. But it's our mission, as the people of God. And there is literally story after story of God using the grittiness and uncomfortableness of Book Club to not only show his love to a bunch of lost men, but to even woo some of these men and bring them to a saving knowledge of Jesus Christ.

To the best of my ability, this is me trying to model hospitality, trying to put myself in a situation where I can be around people who don't believe like me or live like me. And I've seen God bless it and use it to make disciples and push back the darkness.

HOSPITALITY TAKES COURAGE

It may feel that there is a yawning chasm between the extraordinary, cosmic story of what our Warrior God is doing and the idea of inviting folk round for some food. Maybe you are feeling a little underwhelmed with where we have ended up—that courage looks like hospitality. Shouldn't it mainly look like going on marches, or writing our elected representative, or organizing large evangelistic stadium events, or at the very least advocating for Christian morality on social media? Isn't that courageous?

Well, in some ways, it's the big, flashy acts—the kind of stuff we photograph, slap a filter on, and show all our 'friends" online—that get most noticed and yet require the least of us. It's easier to march or write or vent on social media than it is to open up our homes.

Why? First, because missional hospitality is costly. It costs you your time, your money, your comfort. The English have a saying: *A man's home is his castle.* But hospitality demands that you open your door, even when it's inconvenient, rather than pulling up your drawbridge.

Second, missional hospitality is risky. If you are going to show and share the gospel, then you are going to find hostility as well as hunger—and that's hard when it happens in your own home, with your own neighbors.

It costs little to take a hit for the gospel on social media from a friend of a friend who you'll never meet. It is far more of a risk to open yourself up to take that hit from the guy who lives just down the road and who you will see most days for the next years or decades.

Third, missional hospitality requires trust in God instead of ourselves. Marching and writing and debating and organizing feels impressive. After all, these things are the way everyone else seeks to change the world. But when we build friendships and open ourselves up to those who are not like us and do not believe what we do, that feels less impressive and less likely to "work." So it requires us to trust that this is God's way of changing the world.

We have gotten used to the church making big, impressive-sounding statements in the seats of power. But God calls us to make small, counter-cultural statements to those around us. It takes courage to trust that this really is the way God works.

So Christian courage looks like hospitality.

Or, put another way, Christian hospitality demands courage. The extent of your courage will be shown by who sits round your table.

GOING TO WORK WITH DAD

So here it is: courage looks like evangelism, which looks like hospitality—radical, missional hospitality.

It looks like us being committed to greeting everyone, engaging with everyone, making dinner a priority, and, in everything, loving the outsider.

We don't do this to try and gain credibility in our culture. We don't this to be known as nice people. We do this so that we can make the Lord Jesus known.

I can't even put into words the joy that comes from seeing someone sit at your table, ask questions about Jesus, and start to take seriously the faith that you have shown them in your hospitality: to ask you for prayer, to ask if they could come to your church. By God's mercy, if they become a Christian, I want you to know the joy of knowing that God used the home he's given you, the table he's given you, and the food he's given you to reach those around you.

I don't know if you ever got to go to work with your dad when you were a kid. Maybe he gave you a bit of work to do while you were there and you were thinking, *Wow, this is really important, grown-up stuff. I don't even really know what this is, but it's very exciting and it's very serious.* That's a cool day when you're a kid.

Well, hospitality is God's work, and your heavenly Father wants you to come work with him.

God says,

"Hey, I'm saving some folks in your area. Do you want to come
do some eternal work with me?"

And you say,

"Yeah, great. Thanks, Father. What do you want me to do?"

"Well, for starters, see those folk in your neighborhood who
think Christians are narrow-minded, irrelevant jerks? And
see that family who just doesn't really fit in, for whatever
reason? I want you to invite them round, eat dinner with
them, engage with them and listen to them, and love them."

"Dinner? With them? That's what you want me to do?"

"Yes."

"Um. You'll help me, right?"

"Behold, I am with you always, to the end of the age."

7. YOU WERE MADE FOR NOW

This is a great time to be a Christian. Not an easy time—but an exciting one.

I know it doesn't look that way. When I think about our cultural moment, I can't help but see parallels with Christopher Nolan's sinister Batman universe—a society plagued by fear, a society where the line between good and evil has faded, a society marked by skepticism and cynicism, a society with very little hope. It's what the cultural commentator Mark Sayers calls a "non-place"—a culture with no sense of true and meaningful morals, relationships, or identity.

But God's people are called to live by faith, not by sight. And our faith tells us that none of this is an accident.

God didn't have his attention taken from this world for a few decades and then look back to find things had gone off track. God's not sitting around thinking, *Oh, I wonder how this whole thing is going to play out. This whole post-Christian thing has me worried. Let's have a holy Trinity huddle and try to figure it out.*

No, that's not it. The end of Christendom may have surprised and scared many Christians, but it has not taken him aback. Our God is greater than us, and our God is greater than any cultural norm or pressure.

Our God has got this.

When we live by faith in that God, we are freed from living out of fear, whether that's fear over our jobs, our reputation, our children, or our freedom. When we learn to look up more than we look within or look around, so that we put our hope and trust in God, we're unleashed to be bold in and for him. We move beyond seeking to convert the culture, or condemn the culture, or consume the culture. We walk with courage—with a deep, optimistic confidence—for we know how this story ends and we know why we are in this story.

As his people, we get to show our great God to this dark world in how we live and what we say. That's exciting. And God put you—yes, you—here to do just that.

It's no mistake that we've entered the age of unbelief—it's all part of God's plan.

And it's also no mistake that *you* are part of the church in this age of unbelief—that is part of God's plan too.

UNIQUELY WIRED, UNIQUELY PLACED

God has specifically designed you and me, with our particular gifts and personalities and passions, for such a time and place as this.

Psalm 139 says:

"For you formed my inward parts; you knitted me together in my mother's womb. I praise you, for I am fearfully and wonderfully made. Wonderful are your works; my soul knows it very well. My frame was not hidden from you, when I was being made in secret, intricately woven in the depths of the earth. Your eyes saw my unformed substance; in your book were written, every one of them, the days that were formed for me, when as yet there was none of them." (v 13-16)

Throughout the Old Testament, the idea of "frame" is talking about our physical makeup: how we're built. One of the divine activities behind the biological processes that went on in our mothers' wombs is that God was putting us together for the days he would give to us. He was building us for the life he knew he would give to us.

But that's not all, because the psalmist knows that "your eyes saw my unformed substance." That means God wired you in stature. He wired you physically. He wired you emotionally. He wired you with personality: your fight-or-flight response, your harmonizing, your persisting, your achieving. All of that is hardwired into you by God.

You've been uniquely wired by a divine hand. And God doesn't make mistakes. He didn't get distracted while he was knitting you together and drop a stitch.

We're uniquely wired.

And we're uniquely placed:

"The God who made the world and everything in it, being Lord of heaven and earth ... made from one man every nation of mankind to live on all the face of the earth, having determined allotted periods and the boundaries of their dwelling place, that they should seek God, and perhaps feel their way toward him ... He is actually not far from each one of us." (Acts 17 v 24, 26-27)

God made you to worship him and live faithful to him right where you are, right when you are. He is not looking at the age of unbelief and wishing he'd played his A-team for this era, rather than you and me. And knowing that should comfort us. God knows what he's doing.

Knowing that should also eradicate any sense of boredom in our lives. What I mean is this: God is at work behind everything, setting us up as heralds of his good news to everyone. He is at work in our families, our friends, our neighbors, our co-workers, and potentially all those we come in contact with.

None of our conversations and interactions and situations are by chance (Christians don't believe in chance). They are by divine appointment.

God has uniquely wired you with specific gifts and tendencies, and uniquely placed you where you live, work, and play in order to give you unique opportunities to speak to those he's lined up for you to meet about the God who has done all this.

God could have given today's church an Augustine, a Martin Luther, a Jonathan Edwards, an Amy Carmichael, a C.H. Spurgeon, an Elisabeth Elliot, or a [insert your favorite hero from church history here].

But he didn't.

He gave today's church, in this age of unbelief, you and me.

That's our calling. That's our privilege. That's our responsibility.

TAKE HEART

So yes, these are hard days. And yes, they may get worse. Of course, I'm not saying that I want actual persecution and fierce suffering. I'm just saying that if we live through those days, they will not be unique for the church and they will not mean the defeat of the church.

In fact, as we've said, in our age we're back in the place where the church thrives the most—on the margins, being seen as unique and weird.

After all, it was on the margins where Christ lived, died, and rose again. It was on the margins that he built his church. It was on the margins that his church spread like wildfire.

As my friends Steve Timmis and Tim Chester say in *Everyday Church*:

"We can not only survive on the margins; we can thrive on the margins. From the margins we point to God's coming world. We offer an alternative lifestyle, values, relationships—a community that proves incredibly attractive ... as men and women who, like our Savior before us, are those who are marginal yet world changing."

To be that kind of church calls each one of us to live with God-sized courage. And who knows what the Lord may do through his courageous people in this age of unbelief?

So, take heart. We serve a God of infinite riches and knowledge. We are small, but he is able.

Take heart. We live for a God who has fought for us and is fighting for us and will return for us. History has already been decided.

Take heart. We are invited into that story, pushing back the dark with the light of Christ.

Take heart. Christ is risen, and we can stand on his grace and look to his eternity.

Take heart. Wherever you are, God has given you all you need to live with holiness—with integrity, devotion, and evangelistic hospitality.

Take heart. You were, quite literally, made for this moment.

This is a great time to be a Christian.

Take heart.

BIBLIOGRAPHY

Andy Crouch, *Culture Making* (IVP, 2013)

Richard Dawkins, *The God Delusion*
(Houghton Mifflin Harcourt, 2006)

Timothy Keller, *Center Church* (Zondervan, 2012)

Martin Luther King, Jr., *Strength to Love* (Fortress, 2010)

C.S. Lewis, *Mere Christianity* (HarperOne, 2015)

C.S. Lewis, *The Screwtape Letters* (HarperOne, 2015)

Tremper Longman III and Daniel G. Reid, *God is a Warrior*
(Zondervan, 1995)

Stuart Murray, *Post-Christendom: Church and Mission in a
Strange New World* (Paternoster, 2004)

Juan Sanchez, *1 Peter For You*
(The Good Book Company, 2016)

James K.A. Smith, *You Are What You Love* (Brazos, 2016)

Rico Tice, *Honest Evangelism*
(The Good Book Company, 2015)

Steve Timmis & Tim Chester, *Everyday Church*
(Crossway, 2012)

A.W. Tozer, *The Knowledge of the Holy*
(Harper & Brothers, 1961)

ACKNOWLEDGMENTS

This book would not exist if it weren't for The Village Church. We are burdened by this topic, first and foremost, because of our love for the men and women of The Village, and our desire to see our church have an enduring courage and hope in the Lord no matter what comes our way. And it's the elders and leadership of The Village who have graciously given us the opportunity to take what God is up to here, what was born here, and share it with anyone else willing to listen through this book.

There are so many godly, brilliant men and women who have paved the way for this project, helping the church navigate the space between sacred and secular through their teaching and writing. Andy Crouch, James K.A. Smith, Russell Moore, Lecrae, Jon Tyson, Timothy Keller, Stuart Murray, Christian Smith, Alissa Wilkinson, Tremper Longman III, and Daniel G. Reid are just a few of those individuals. We feel like we can't take any credit for this work, but owe everything to these gifted folks, as well as to our editor, Carl Laferton, and the team at The Good Book Company.

And none of this would have happened if it weren't for our spouses and our families. They are a gift and a grace. This ministry is a partnership, and we are better together because of their gifts and their love for the church.

thegoodbook
COMPANY

BIBLICAL | RELEVANT | ACCESSIBLE

At The Good Book Company, we are dedicated to helping Christians and local churches grow. We believe that God's growth process always starts with hearing clearly what he has said to us through his timeless word—the Bible.

Ever since we opened our doors in 1991, we have been striving to produce resources that honor God in the way the Bible is used. We have grown to become an international provider of user-friendly resources to the Christian community, with believers of all backgrounds and denominations using our Bible studies, books, evangelistic resources, DVD-based courses, and training events.

We want to equip ordinary Christians to live for Christ day by day, and churches to grow in their knowledge of God, their love for one another, and the effectiveness of their outreach.

Call us for a discussion of your needs or visit one of our local websites for more information on the resources and services we provide.

Your friends at The Good Book Company

NORTH AMERICA
UK & EUROPE
AUSTRALIA
NEW ZEALAND

thegoodbook.com
thegoodbook.co.uk
thegoodbook.com.au
thegoodbook.co.nz

866 244 2165
0333 123 0880
(02) 9564 3555
(+64) 3 343 2463

WWW.CHRISTIANITYEXPLORED.ORG
Our partner site is a great place for those exploring the Christian faith, with a clear explanation of the good news, powerful testimonies and answers to difficult questions.